You're Getting Older, So What?

You're Getting Older, So What?
By Ruth Turk

Foreword by Margaret Chase Smith
Former United States Senator

Illustrations by John Livesay

HERALD PUBLISHING HOUSE
Independence, Missouri

Library of Congress Cataloging in Publication Data

Turk, Ruth, 1917-
   You're getting older, so what?

   Bibliography: p.
   1. Retirement—United States. 2. Aging.
   3. Old age. I. Title.
   HQ1064.U5T87   301.43′5   76-39989
   ISBN 0-8309-0166-3

Printed in the United States of America

DEDICATION

TO
my husband, Len, whose love and
understanding has helped me put
it all together

CONTENTS

FOREWORD

I consider Ruth Turk's book to be must reading for almost everyone fifty years of age and over—that is fifty years young and over. It can really make the difference between happiness and desolation.

Retirement is too often viewed as a time when people are put out to pasture to prepare themselves for death. Too seldom is it recognized for the great opportunity that it gives us to literally live again and to do the many things we have wanted so long to do but simply didn't have the time or freedom to do.

Age is really not a matter of chronology but rather a matter of attitude. I have known some people who were born with a sixty-five-year-old attitude.

I was retired from the United States Senate involuntarily by a narrow margin of the voters because of my age—the only issue my successful opponent openly admitted that he had against me. Frankly, it was a shock to me—but not to the extent that I just faded away as my enemies had expected. Rather it turned out to be a blessing in disguise, because instead of crying myself to death I picked myself up and entered a new and glorious field of activity—the world of academe where my associates were predominantly students and academicians many years my junior. I would not trade places in the Senate for it now even if I had the chance.

The importance of the message of Ruth Turk's book cannot be overstated. She says it interestingly, practically, and effectively. It is solid gold in reassurance, comfort, and exploring new horizons.

Margaret Chase Smith
Former United States Senator

ACKNOWLEDGMENTS

The idea of writing this book did not flower overnight. It materialized as a result of becoming part of a totally unexpected experience—growing older in a community of one's peers and discovering how wonderful it can be. With so many vague and negative notions on aging floating around, the desire to share my personal reactions with the world could no longer be denied. Yet, after discussion with my most loving critic and partner—my husband—I realized that such a book would certainly not reflect *every* kind of aging in the twentieth century. A complete book on the subject would include how the wealthy upper class ages as well as the indigent lower class. Inasmuch as I can speak honestly only of the class with which I am most familiar, I deal essentially with the feelings and problems of the middle class.

I am grateful, therefore, to all those delightful middle-class people who helped make this book a reality—my friends, neighbors, and students in the community known as Century Village in West Palm Beach, Florida, and to the readers of my "Ask Ruth" and "Rap with Ruth" newspaper columns who did not hesitate to share their problems and experiences with me and the other residents of Palm Beach County.

I am also indebted to Dr. George Fitzelle at the University of Rhode Island in Kingston, Rhode Island, who was my first instructor in a course in gerontology some years ago (in which, incidentally, I thought I was the oldest student); to Dr. Phillip Taietz at Cornell University, Ithaca, New York, who encouraged me to discuss the idea for this book with him last summer; and to Lorena McCray, Ann Neugenboren, Ruth Zeiger, Judy Atkin, and Claire Braun for cheerfully taking part in one of the most onerous burdens of completing a manuscript—typing!

INTRODUCTION—THE ROCKING CHAIR MYTH

Let's face it—our parents and grandparents were sold down the river by a chilling and firmly established myth. If they lived long enough they were going to end up, helpless and inactive, in a rocking chair. There are people of this generation who *still* believe it, despite constantly growing evidence to the contrary. With all the emphasis on beautiful people under thirty, is it any wonder that those approaching forty work frantically at squeezing every last drop out of living because they can't believe anything worthwhile can happen at fifty, sixty, seventy, or beyond?

Well, I have news for these worriers which may *not* be news to those lucky ones of my generation who have discovered that "it just ain't so." You don't have to dry up and sink into the ground just because you're getting older. You don't have to head for the rocking chair because your parents did, or because television and other public media constantly stress the joys of youth, sex, and physical vigor. You don't have to retire to shuffleboard, memories, and baby-sitting just because you're sixty-five or more. You can have an even more rewarding life-style in your sixties than you ever had in your thirties if you want to. How do I know? Because I'm doing it, along with a lot of other people who are growing older and saying, "So what?"

A few years ago I "dropped out" of a harried, tension-provoking situation as a teacher in a big city school system, where I had become little more than a policewoman without a uniform. It was with some trepidation that we moved into a southern retirement community to find out what it was all about. My mental reservation was that at the first sight of a rocking chair I would run as fast as my very agile legs would carry me. Some five years later I am still using my still very agile legs to keep moving in every direction, and I have yet to see a rocking chair anywhere in the distance!

Much to my delight and excitement, I have found that I am a part of a new breed—a pioneer generation, perhaps, but nevertheless a whole new group in American middle-class society that is growing older and doing its own thing. The rocking chair is being used strictly as a decorative antique in the homes of this pioneer generation, and it's rocked only when it gets dusted or polished.

Since people are living longer, they are no longer content to be relegated to the land of the living dead just because they have some gray hairs, a few liver spots, or extra lines in their faces. They are learning that, provided they maintain good physical health, a positive attitude and interest in life, and a confidence

16

toward their place in the scheme of things, there is another stage of life that can be even more meaningful than the earlier ones. Retirement no longer means retirement *from life* for many people these days.

For me, it has meant retirement from one phase of living into another one, only this one has greater flexibility and fewer limitations than all of the previous ones. Most women and men of my generation were bogged down by the pressures of school competition, marriage, child-rearing, career and job problems, financial hurdles, parent support, housing, generation gaps, social, sexual, and political bewilderment. We were caught between the rigid apprehension of our elders and the groping experimentation of our sons and daughters. Only in the past decade are we beginning to emerge into the dawn of a new day and find that older people have a lot going for them.

This does not mean that retired people live in a Shangri-la with no problems of any kind. They continue to have problems just as individuals of every generation do, but the new breed of retiree is reacting and coping with a spirit and confidence unknown to their elders.

A fantastic example of a new kind of retirement community is the one we chose in which to find another way of life. My first step was to file for teacher certification in the state of Florida. Somewhere in the back of my mind floated the rocking chair legend that somehow would not be denied. And so I was interviewed by a number of school principals who tactfully concealed their surprise that I should wish to reenter the field after leaving it. Despite my youthful appearance, it was apparent they felt I should be content to take on a more appropriate "hobby." Like what? Crocheting or backgammon? I recall leaving the last interview with a sense of relief. Unknowingly at that moment I had been freed.

From that day to the present, I have been truly free in a way I never thought possible. It has not been "retirement" in the outmoded sense of the word. It has become a vital, involved stage I like to call "refirement."

In that first stage I moved to encourage a group of residents in our condominium complex to join me in discussions about their problems. Basking in the warm, relaxing atmosphere of Florida's winter sunshine, one after another formerly reserved person started to open up. All sorts of problems emerged— problems about leisure, health, sex, relationships between husbands and wives, community recognition, care of aged parents, problems of widows and widowers, concern about married children, unmarried children and grandchildren, economic values, new friendships, and a host of others. It was obvious that my neighbors had definitely *not* retired from living. They had all kinds of plans not only for the present but for the future. It was while I sat in that semicircle of enthusiastic, communicating people that I realized where my own future lay.

People all around me were living longer and were definitely interested in living better. How could they go about it? They had taken the first step. They were thinking and talking about it, no longer accepting the ancient stereotypes of the bent head, the cane, and the rocking chair.

And so when I received an offer to teach courses in "You're Getting Older—and Better" in Palm Beach County's Community Education Department I accepted with a sense of excitement and purpose. Having had several years experience as an instructor in the Century Village Clubhouse in West Palm Beach as well as a background of courses and research at various universities, I had no qualms about motivating my contemporaries in their search for some of the answers. I refused to climb onto the lecture platform, although I received offers, because it was my feeling that these rap sessions would be more successful in an informal, living-room setting. I did agree to write several local columns, one of which was called, "Ask Ruth." When the anonymous letters started pouring in, I realized that here indeed was a need for people to air the problems of adjustment to growing older in modern society.

It was then that the idea for this book was born. Since I had inadvertently become a "Dear Abby" of the retirement set, it seemed feasible that this was the time to share these problems with all segments of a society growing older every day. Furthermore, this also presented an opportunity, not only to dispel the whole rocking chair myth but to consider, mull over, and suggest some practical ways of getting better as we get older.

To this end, I have included some of the letters and comments received from the readers of the "Ask Ruth" column to indicate the kinds of concerns people have in retirement. Certainly they are not conclusive of all types of retirees, but they do present a picture— sometimes negative but always realistic. Above all, it shows them as thinking, feeling, involved, concerned, and very much *alive*. In one way or the other, they seem to be repeating, "Of course, I'm growing older—so what?"

If I can infect the readers of this book with the same

anticipation, delight, and excitement I feel as I grow older, I will be well rewarded for the time spent on it. If I can reassure any young person brave enough to pick up this book that the best is yet to come, I will be well rewarded. Most important, if I can influence a number of aging skeptics to join me in saying every day of their lives, "I *am* getting older—so what?" I will have accomplished the main purpose of this book.

CHAPTER I

TO RETIRE OR NOT TO RETIRE—that is the question

The fear of retirement has kept many men and women on a nine-to-five job until they were virtually forced out. The terrifying image of a decrepit person peering through a window at the world has haunted people approaching sixty-five because this was all with which they were familiar. Although the actual truth of the matter is that individuals age at different rates whether they retire or not, until a relatively short time ago the myths persisted. The outstanding one was that people who retired were at the end of the line. Consequently, few retired voluntarily, and even fewer prepared for this stage. Occasionally, a spouse encouraged his or her partner to leave it all, with the following results.

> *Dear Ruth:*
> *My wife persuaded me to sell my business and retire to Florida even though I felt I was not ready for retirement.*

*She said we would make up for the many years of
hard work and unpleasant conditions of living in a large,
crowded city. She painted such a beautiful picture of
leisure living that I finally agreed, even though I had
always imagined that only very sick or old people are
forced to retire.*

*Now after almost two years, I find that my worst
fears are being realized. This life is boring and pointless because I haven't anything worthwhile to do. When
I ran my business, I was "on the go" from morning
to night.*

*Now the hours and days drag by and every day is
like Sunday, so I haven't anything to look forward to.
Eating, sleeping, playing cards, taking long walks or
sitting around the pool is not my "cup of tea." I am
ready to return to the Big Town, but my wife begs
me to give it more time.*

*Will six months or a year make any difference if
my environment remains the same?*

Not Ready

Dear Not Ready:

*I don't blame you for not wishing to commit
"emotional suicide."*

*Perhaps you were not completely ready, but then,
you may never be ready unless you do something
about yourself rather than your present environment.*

*If you can begin to see this way of life not as
a retirement from living but simply the way to a new
and even more stimulating stage of life, you will have
no need to change environments.*

*If you want to be "on the go from morning to
night" and are in good health, there is no reason why
you can't be. It is no longer true that only very sick
or old people have retirement wished on them. Sensible
younger people are beginning to plan for retirement
long before the actual day.*

*Instead of plunging back into the hectic routine you
once knew, why not become involved in a project*

or purpose which will occupy your time and energy?
After all, you can now do anything or be anything
you have always wanted to do or be. Stop thinking
about yourself and start thinking about others. There are
numerous civic, political, cultural, and social outlets in
your community which will welcome you with
open arms.

Whatever you do—don't run away from yourself!

The following letter came from a man who was more concerned with the *geographic* location of retirement than anything else. Certainly it is important to investigate different areas. We are partial to southern Florida ourselves because of the delightful winter climate, but we found that adjustments had to be made, such as leaving when the summers made us uncomfortable, etc. This sometimes is an unpredictable factor, since even summers in semitropical climates are not intolerable for some people. It is desirable to maintain a measure of flexibility, if at all possible, in living arrangements. If that is not feasible, it is amazing how secondary the "where" becomes when the "why" and "how" are satisfying.

Dear Ruth:
I live in a large northern city and have not yet
retired. A Florida friend of mine sent me a copy of
your column because he thinks you can help me with
my problem.
I will be sixty-five years old next year and plan to
retire at that time. I'm not looking forward to it for
a very simple but upsetting reason. I don't know where to
go when I retire.

25

I don't want to remain in this city because retired people here become "prisoners" when cold weather sets in. It's also not safe for an older person to go out for a walk after dark.

I've done some research on retirement areas and come up with very frustrating results! California has fog and earthquakes, Florida has bugs, Oregon has lots of rain, and Arizona is much too hot.

Where can a retired person live in peace, happiness, and safety—or am I asking for the "impossible"?

Frustrated Fred

Dear Frustrated Fred:

I don't believe you are asking for the impossible, but perhaps you are not taking a realistic approach to the "where" of retirement.

It's a fact that no climate in the world is perfect at all times of the year. It is also a fact that no large city in the world today is absolutely safe at all times for all people before or after dark. However, there are a number of retired people who enjoy the life of their community, wherever it happens to be. If you are going to fret and worry about the quirks of nature such as fog, rain, heat, cold, and bugs, you may have a serious problem settling anywhere on this planet!

Perhaps it might be a sensible idea to concentrate on some of the other facets of retirement. Surely some of your friends can reassure you that when you are active and involved in retirement, your physical surroundings take on that much less importance.

I am not negating creature comfort completely. What I am saying is that, after all, you have to take yourself wherever you go. You will find peace and happiness when you have friends and something to look forward to every day of your life.

Concentrate on a few important goals and plans for your future retirement—then perhaps the place where you work out these plans and goals will be that much easier to decide on.

Another example of a viewpoint based on a short visit to a retirement area is expressed vigorously by a woman who calls herself "Snowbird." I empathize with her because I recall that my first visit to a popular retirement community also induced an unpleasant reaction. When making a complete change, I found it wise to spend a good deal of time and thought on a final choice. *Living* in a certain atmosphere for any length of time gives a much better picture of the community than a brief visit. There is no question but that the removal of old friends and family for some people is a traumatic experience and must be carefully considered. Many retirees remain in the same city where they have worked and enjoy the advantages it has to offer, which they couldn't do before.

Dear Ruth:

I belong in the category popularly known as "snow-birds," and frankly I prefer it that way!

We live in a northern city most of the year and come down for a few weeks at a time when we want a change of climate. However, I don't see what's so great about living in a condominium in a retirement area as a total way of life. As a matter of fact, I think there's something downright unhealthy and maybe abnormal about removing yourself from family, friends, and everything important. I could understand it for health reasons, but why a happy, well-adjusted person should want to crowd together with people all his own age in an unreal Shangri la is beyond me! I feel there is something pathetic about older people constantly swimming, playing golf, cards, and other games as a substitute for involvement.

Recently, my husband who sided with me in my feeling about condominium retirement seems to be undergoing a change of heart. His argument is that if so many of our friends and acquaintances are doing it,

it must be worthwhile. Do I have to accept a way of life
that is disagreeable to me just because friends seem to
like it?

Snowbird

Dear Snowbird:

People contemplating retirement select different areas
and ways of living for any number of reasons. Some
may be influenced by what their friends are doing,
but this is rather risky, since values and goals are not
identical, even in retirement. It is important to evaluate
what you want most from life as you grow older. If
this is what you are doing, you are to be commended for
using your own mind rather than blindly following a
popular trend.

In recent years, there has been a movement toward
removal from colder to warmer climates and to more
leisurely styles of living for those older people who can
afford it. As a snowbird, you probably are not receiving
a complete picture of the Shangri la you observe for
short periods. To those condominium residents who
merely "swim, play golf, cards, and other games"
it is involvement enough for them. (Perhaps they are also
snowbirds on well-earned vacations.) There is nothing to
keep those who wish to be more vigorously involved
from engaging in more challenging pursuits. There are
many retirees who use their leisure in contributing
politically, culturally, and socially to their respective
communities, despite the fact that they may be housed
in condominium residences. As for "crowding together"
with people all in the same age category, there is more
than one explanation for this phenomenon. To live in a
group of one's own peers is to provide emotional
security and comfort to the individual. It is easier
to share joys and sorrows with those your own age
who are going through the same kinds of experiences
at the same time. On the other hand, there are those
who feel keenly the loss of family and old-friend
relationships and are not compensated by more salubrious
climates and freer modes of existence.

There is no question that you do not need to accept something which appears disagreeable, but you apparently enjoy at least one part of this way of life. In view of how your husband now feels, perhaps you should consider a trial period of at least one year before definitely making up your mind about any permanent arrangement in retirement.

And then there is the person who feels like a "fish out of water." Though there are others like him, he feels as if *he* is the only one. Getting older has little to do with doing your own thing, no matter what it happens to be. More and more of the new generation of retirees are becoming aware of this and doing something about it. Frequently it is necessary to search for the kind of colony where residents have interests similar to your own. Sometimes it is a challenge to remain where you are and proclaim your individuality, just as you did when you were younger. Or if you never did such a thing when you were younger, why *not* start now?

Dear Ruth:
I'm beginning to feel like "a fish out of water" in the retirement area where I live. When I occasionally confide some of my inner thoughts to some of my neighbors, I meet with polite silence, a puzzled smile, or a skeptical remark. My wife tells me that I am not realistic and should start acting my age, like everyone around me.
Somehow I can't accept the fact that now that I am retired I am not expected to accomplish anything unusual or remarkable. When I worked and supported

*a family, I could not take the time to do something
just for myself. When I had a day off, I was too tired
to do anything except socialize with friends.*

*Now that I have all the time in the world to
socialize and have fun, I find it's not enough for me.
I want to contribute something to the world. I don't
know exactly what.*

*Am I too old to write a book, create a sculpture,
build a monument, develop a new scientific theory or
invention? Or should I just relax around the pool
like most of my retired friends and leave the great things
of the world to the younger generation?*

Fish-Out-of-Water

Dear Fish-Out-of-Water:

*If most of your friends just relax around the pool
and do very little else, it's small wonder that you feel
like a fish out of water! This may be enough for
some people in some retirement areas, but this doesn't
mean that all retired people agree that a meaningful
life belongs only to the younger generation.*

*There is no need for you to accept any of the
stereotypes about getting older, especially if you feel you
have something to offer. After all, Albert Schweitzer still
felt there was something more for him to do at age
eighty-six; Charles Chaplin continued to produce
pictures at age seventy-five; Pablo Picasso at age eighty-
five said, "It takes a long time to become young";
Pearl S. Buck, author of eighty-four books, declared on
her eightieth birthday, "I have so much more to do!"
Helen Hayes, distinguished actress, commented at age
seventy, "It's such a wasted effort to try to turn back the
clock when there's so much to be done."*

*Avoid disclosing your secret hopes and dreams to those
who will only be baffled and upset. Your goals, strange as
they may appear to some of your retired contemporaries,
are not only ambitious but admirable.*

*If you have the desire to make an outstanding
contribution to society before you grow older, don't
let anyone or anything stop you! You may not become a*

Schweitzer or a Picasso, but you will give something
of yourself to others in your own way.

And if you are not comfortable swimming in the same
water with unsympathetic fish, you may eventually have
to change the kind of fish you swim with—or the water
you're swimming in.

━━━━━

No one formula works for all retirees. Even with the new breed, some people choose to withdraw from activity, just as their parents or grandparents may have done. Many studies have shown, however, that such persons tend to age more rapidly than those who get involved.

Dear Ruth:

I am annoyed with retirement communities that won't
leave people alone and constantly try to draw them into
all kinds of stupid activities.

I have worked hard my whole life; now I want some
peace and quiet. Above all, I don't feel like singing,
making things with my hands, gossiping with neighbors
at the pool, working on committees, or pitching horse-
shoes. I purposely selected an area which didn't permit
pets and children, but I now find some adults who are
worse than either of them!

Don't get me wrong, please—I don't
hate people, but I want to do what I feel like
doing when I want to. Is there something wrong in a
person wanting to retire in the original sense of the word?
Or am I abnormal because I enjoy the privacy of my
home and refuse to take part in a bunch of foolish,
time-passing "activities" dreamed up by busy organizers?

Happy Hermit

Dear Happy Hermit:

You sound more like an unhappy *hermit!*

If you really wanted to be a hermit, you certainly didn't do very effective research on many retirement communities. If you had, you might have learned that such communities generally aim at providing older people with activities and program which will keep them healthy and involved.

Many medical authorities and gerontologists appear to agree that planned daily activities are necessary for people who retire without any plans of their own. Also, in those retirement areas where such highly organized programs exist, the residents are paying for the privilege of enjoying them.

You certainly are entitled to the peace and quiet you seek, but perhaps your particular choice of home at this time is not quite the right one for you. Sometimes, in the first stages of retirement, it is not unusual for a person who has worked hard all his life to want to withdraw and contemplate his soul in tranquillity. The chances are that after enough solitude, you may want to rejoin your friends and neighbors and share in some of the things they seem to enjoy so much.

Retirement, as originally defined by Webster, meant a withdrawal from circulation or a retreat into seclusion. The study of south Florida retirement complexes belies this definition for the most part today. However there is nothing "abnormal" in wanting to do your own thing, no matter what the books, the experts, or your neighbors say.

There are a number of retired people who have no need of organized activities; they are able to pursue their own interests quietly and happily. You have no need to feel guilty at being a private person. I would suggest, however, that you occasionally join a committee with a worthwhile purpose or make something with your hands, if only to discover whether you may possibly be missing something.

Although I have found that getting involved all over again has been one of the most exciting and unexpected developments of this stage of my life, I don't think an authoritative dogma should be forced on any retiree. There are varying life-styles both before and after retirement; therefore it is difficult to adequately define so broad a term as "successful retirement."

Dear Ruth:

What do you consider really "successful" adjustment to retirement?

I am puzzled by all the different types of retired people I've been coming across since I recently retired myself. Some of them seem happy, active, and well-adjusted; they are constantly doing things and going places. Other of my neighbors keep to themselves, refuse to get involved in social and community affairs, yet they, too, act satisfied with their way of life. A few others (fortunately, I haven't met very many) seem bitter, upset, disgruntled, and miserable with themselves, their spouses, and practically everyone they meet. I've also noticed that many women seem to be better adjusted to retirement life than men.

What causes such different responses to the adjustment of retirement, and which kind is the most "normal"?

Recently Retired

Dear Recently Retired:

So-called "successful" adjustment to retirement is defined in different ways, according to who is conducting the research. The way a man or woman grows older depends to a degree on his personality—on what his psychological drives are and his ability to satisfy them as he ages. Personality has an important effect on whether a person grows older smoothly and on how he goes about it.

Some people move tranquilly into retirement because

33

they are relatively free of neurotic conflicts, are able to accept themselves realistically, and find genuine satisfaction in activities and relationships. Feeling their lives have been rewarding, they are able to grow older without regret for the past or loss in the present. They take aging for granted and make the most of it. Another group who are rather passive and inactive welcome the opportunity to be free of responsibility and to indulge their passive needs in aging. Some people work consciously at warding off as much physical and mental decline as they can possibly manage, finding security in projects, hobbies, volunteer work, and other interests. The few really miserable ones you refer to are usually those who have failed to achieve their goals earlier in life, blamed others for their disappointments, and are unable to accept the challenges of growing older gracefully. Poor adjustment to retirement among those disgruntled people seems to stem from a combination of lifelong personality problems, ill health, and/or economic factors.

A prevailing view has been that happy retired people are mostly those who participate actively in everything that goes on. Sharply differing from this view is the theory that other persons age successfully by withdrawing from social roles. Studies in gerontology indicate that differences in status, income, occupation, and cultural background also have important influences on how successful is the adjustment to retirement.

As far as the better adjustment of women is concerned, some researchers indicate this may have something to do with the fact that most women have had considerably more experience in this area than most men—that is they have been "retired" at home so much longer. Different responses are to be expected at this stage of life just as at any other stage, simply because people are always different fron one another, no matter how old they are. Who is to say what is "normal" aging? And if you are happy, and make those around you happy, who cares?

Some of the most beautiful and unsolicited testimonials came from students in my discussion groups. Because I believe that more of the positive aspects of getting older, whether retired or not, should be stressed by society in general, and by the fulfilled individuals themselves, I am including comments by some of these individuals.

Jerry, age sixty-seven, retired five years:

> *I am really getting to know my wife. For the first time in our lives we are doing things together we never had a chance to do before.*

Anne, age sixty-two, retired two years:

> *We are taking cross-country trips like a couple of kids. I never dreamed it could be such fun.*

Dora, age sixty-four, retired four years:

> *Although I miss my children from time to time, I have a marvelous sense of freedom—as if there's a whole new life ahead of me.*

Bill, age seventy-one, retired six years:

> *If I had known ten years ago what I know now, I wouldn't have been so afraid to retire. I'm sorry I waited until I was sixty-five, but I'm making up for lost time.*

Jean, age sixty-one, retired one year:

> *When my husband passed away, I thought my life was over, too. But I am so busy doing volunteer work in the hospitals and nursing homes with people so much less fortunate than I am, that I have forgotten how lonely I was.*

George, age sixty-nine, retired four years:

Who ever dreamed I would become an artist at this stage of the game? I never held a brush in my hand until three years ago. Now a day seldom passes that I don't spend several hours at my easel.

CHAPTER II

BRIDGING THE GAPS

The term "generation gap" which became popular some years ago referred exclusively to two generations. The truth is that many gaps exist not only between generations but within the generations and between people of all ages and stages. Since people are living longer, more gaps are beginning to appear. With the advent of earlier retirement and the development of the young-old pioneer generation, people are confronted by unexpected problems.

One of the most severe readjustments for a married couple in retirement is the acceptance of continuous confrontation. As long as the opportunities for contact were limited and each spouse was familiar with his or her role demands, the union was successful. With freedom, unlimited time at their disposal, and frequently no plans or preparation for the future, husband and wife are bewildered by their own particular "gap." One of my readers wrote:

Dear Ruth:

I thought when we retired I would have as much leisure time as my husband. Instead, I find I am preparing three meals a day instead of one. I used to have a cleaning girl; now I do all my own housework. Instead of inviting friends once in a while, it seems that we are always entertaining either neighbors or friends or relatives who think we are running a hotel resort.

Is it fair for only a husband to retire? Shouldn't the wife have an equal amount of leisure? And if the wife is also to be fully retired, who will clean, cook, shop, entertain, etc.?

Working Wife

Dear Working Wife:

It looks as if Women's Lib has infiltrated the world of retirement! You do not indicate how much leisure time your husband has, but I would assume that he could probably spare a few hours a week to enter into an agreeable arrangement for both of you. If he is willing to pitch in once or twice a week to help in general housecleaning, this would free you both to enjoy more time pursuing a new project or hobby. Perhaps eating some meals out together would provide a delightful interlude and a change from home cooking. It might also be worthwhile to share the shopping and entertaining chores by dividing the lists so that each one of you is free at least part of the time. There is nothing wrong in tactfully allowing visiting neighbors, friends, and relatives to know that, although you enjoy seeing them on occasion, you also enjoy this newfound relationship with your husband in retirement. If you are subtle but firm they will get the message. You, as well as your spouse, should certainly be free to lead full, happy lives in retirement without hurting each other or anyone else.

And there is the baffled husband who retired but found that his wife preferred to remain in her secretarial position rather than "joining" him. It is clear that the husband had fixed ideas prior to retirement, expecting his wife to fall smoothly into line with his plans.

> *Dear Ruth:*
>
> *How can a married couple enjoy a satisfactory life when the husband is retired and the wife continues to work?*
>
> *I worked hard all my life at a six-day-a-week job and felt I earned the rewards of retirement. When I retired my wife stayed on at her job as private secretary to an important man. She said she would retire as soon as her boss could find a replacement for her. That was two years ago! I don't know how hard my wife's boss has tried to replace her, but it's obvious that she enjoys the prestige and activity of her job.*
>
> *I love my wife and have complete confidence in her. She insists that she loves me also but says she cannot face the boredom of a retired housewife's routine. We have been married a long time, but unless we can find some other way, we may have to consider divorce as a solution. Please help us to return to the happy arrangement we had before I retired.*
>
> *Harried Husband*

> *Dear Harried:*
>
> *Although I sympathize with your predicament, I find your last statement most revealing.*
>
> *You say that you had a "happy arrangement" before you retired. In other words, you did not think about your wife's situation while you were busy working six days a week. You just didn't have the time or energy, probably. But your wife had to find the time and energy after a full day at the office to become a housewife every day, including Sundays. You certainly*

41

*have been patient waiting for her to join you in re-
tirement for two years. Perhaps the thought of what
her "new" role would be is keeping her clinging
tenaciously to her secretarial job!*

*Divorce is never a solution when a couple have been
married a long time, love each other, and want to
work out a mutual problem.*

*Have you considered returning to work yourself on
a part- or full-time basis until your wife really wants to
retire? Or you might present such an exciting picture of
the challenges of retirement to your wife that she will
make certain her boss replaces her immediately.*

*Or, just to be sure, get a good look at her boss and
try to figure our what he's got that possibly you may
be missing. . . and can probably do something about!*

Although I did receive more mail from women than
men, I found that frequently a retired man expressed
himself more freely than he might have before. In our
group discussions, men also spoke up sometimes quite
heatedly about the "gap" that was developing between
them and their spouses. In a number of instances, the
husband was content with things the way they were
and could not understand the need to change after
so many years.

Dear Ruth:

*My wife and I have been married for thirty-seven
years, but we actually spent very little time together.
I left for business before she got up in the morning
and came home late every night after closing the store. I
had time only to eat, watch television, and go to bed.*

On weekends I needed to sleep late to compensate

for the sleep I missed all week. My wife was very
cooperative, understanding, and never complained.

Since we have retired she wants me to change my
old habits, but it's not working out. I still enjoy sleeping
late and watching television in the evenings. I can't see
why I should have to rush around now that I have all
the time in the world. My wife insists that this is wrong.

I don't mind if she does whatever she wants to, but
she feels we should spend more time together in
retirement. If things worked well for thirty-seven years,
is there any reason to change at this point?

Creature of Habit

Dear Creature:

Have you been involved in a marriage or a business
deal for thirty-seven years?

Marriage is usually defined as a mutual relationship
or intimate union between two people (although in recent
years it has taken on varying forms and aspects).

Your wife may have been cooperative for nearly four
decades for economic and psychological reasons she
found easier to accept than to question. In any case
you are fortunate to have had a spouse able to carry on
uncomplainingly for so many years. Most women not
only would find such a relationship rough going but
would do something about it.

In retirement you have been given a wonderful
opportunity to reevaluate and redeem the drab schedule
of your former existence. Your wife indicates that she
still cares for you and wants to get to know you before
it is too late. If you are in good health certainly you
do not require all the extra sleep and television
relaxation (you thought) you needed when you worked.

Since you spent "very little time together," don't
you think this would be an excellent chance to have a
little fun with the girl you married? And if you really
love that girl, maybe you ought to "mind" her doing
whatever she wants to! It might be advisable to
remember that you both *have* retired, and you both

should make the most of the rest of your years together.

*This doesn't mean that you have to "rush around"
or go to extremes if you don't feel up to it. Thinking
you have "all the time in the world" does not give you
a valid excuse to throw away thirty-seven perfectly
"good" (?) years of marriage!*

———

Although the gaps among married couples seem to
concern the partners most, some of the other gaps that
surface as people grow older are also noteworthy. Even
those parents who had moved to other parts of the
country continued to communicate with children and
grandchildren and found themselves constantly involved one way or the other.

Dear Ruth:

*We recently received quite a shock when our daughter
and son-in-law informed us that they had decided to try
a new life-style they called "open marriage." They have
been married five years and have no children. We are
too upset and embarrassed to ask them to explain what
"open marriage" means. When we tried to bring up the
subject with some of our friends, they laughed and said
it was too late for people our age to become interested
in anything like that! Now we are really curious as
well as concerned.*

*We should appreciate your comments and information
on "open marriage" in a future column.*

Mr. and Mrs. Old-fashioned

Dear Old-fashioneds:

*To start with, let me allay your fears in regard to
your children's new life-style. "Open marriage" is not
illegal; it is simply an honest and open relationship*

between two married people based on the equal freedom and identity of both partners. It involves a verbal, intellectual, and emotional commitment to the right of each to grow as an individual. In this kind of marriage, neither person dominates the other. The relationship is based on mutual liking and trust, learning opportunity for growth, and new experiences outside the marriage. The union becomes richer and stronger because it does not stifle the partners; rather it encourages each one to do his/her own thing.

The opposite of open marriage is closed marriage; the latter style has been the one most commonly accepted by generations of couples prior to your daughter and son-in-law's generation. In a closed marriage the ideal is for two individuals to be fused into a single entity—a couple. The wife has a very specific role and so does the husband, ordained by biological and cultural limits. In an open marriage, the Victorian idea of marriage as a gilded cage is completely unacceptable; the relationship thrives on change, flexibility, and true understanding. It is a kind of expanded monogamy, retaining the fulfilling aspects of an intimate, in-depth relationship with another yet eliminating the restrictions formerly believed to be an integral part of monogamy.

If your children are deciding to investigate a new marriage style, it is probably because they are disillusioned with the old one and love each other enough to keep working at their marriage. They also are intelligent enough to do this before children appear on the scene to complicate the situation. If you are really interested in learning more about this fascinating subject read the well-written book by Nena and George O'Neill, Open Marriage. Then you will be able not only to discuss this with the young couple if you wish but to inform your laughing friends that it's never too late to try something new at any age.

Grandparents are sometimes confronted with a situation for which they are unprepared. The following problem was indicative of a huge gap existing among three generations.

Dear Ruth:

Recently our seventeen-year-old granddaughter came to spend the holidays with us. She had written beforehand to ask if she could bring a friend. Of course we said the friend would be welcome. Imagine our reaction when the friend turned out to be a young man of twenty! When we tactfully (we thought) made up a couch for the friend in the living room, they both looked at us as if we were crazy. When they left, my granddaughter told us she had never expected us to be so far "behind the times"! What should "modern" grandparents do when faced with such a situation?

Behind-the-Times

Dear Behind-the-Times:

I don't think "modern" grandparents would do any differently than you did, no matter how antiquated your granddaughter thinks your standards are. If you were really out of step, you might have sent your "precocious" grandchild back home as fast as possible. You showed not only great tact and courtesy toward the young man but unusual tolerance and love for your granddaughter in accepting the situation to the best of your ability. However, if you haven't already done so, I would suggest that you have a discussion not only with your granddaughter but with her parents at your earliest opportunity. The possibility exists that the parents do not know their daughter as well as they should. In any case, it is unfair to place long-distance grandparents in such an untenable situation.

Even though many grandparents and parents of the new breed no longer remain in the same neighborhoods or towns where their families live, they find themselves reacting almost as if they were close by. With greater mobility and fewer financial burdens they may settle in different parts of the country or travel, but they continue to care about what's happening to their children and children's children.

Dear Ruth:

I thought this was the time of life when we would think only of ourselves and not be upset by the problems of our grown children. However I find that I am reacting very strongly to my daughter's life-style, even though she does not live in the same city I do. She lived with one young man for a few months and when they decided to "split" she moved in with another male friend. My daughter was brought up in a respectable home and, though I love her, I cannot understand why she is so casual about her relationships. When I talk to her about it she tells me that the world is "different" today, etc. How can I stop feeling concern about my daughter's way of life?

Aggravated Mother

Dear Aggravated:

There is no way a parent, retired and living in another city or not, will ever feel completely removed from an offspring's "problem." You do not mention your daughter's age, but I assume she is an independent adult. Apparently she is seeking to find herself and doing it in her own way, unconventional and baffling as it may seem to you. Flitting from one arrangement to another may be symptomatic of unrest, insecurity, curiosity, or loneliness. She may be doing what she thinks is the "thing" to do as a liberated woman in the latter part of the twentieth century. On the other hand, what appears to be "casual" to you may be meaningful to her. Although you feel concern, it might be helpful

47

*to realize that eventually she may want a more stable
and permanent relationship. The best you can do at this
time is to leave the lines of communication open.
Let her know that, although you do not care for
her present life-style, you will keep on loving her and
wanting her to be happy. Since you are retired and
living in another city, you have already removed yourself—at least physically—from the situation.*

────────────

Gaps exist not only in the relationships between families but crop up among friends and neighbors who are unprepared for their new way of life. Recognition in the eyes of peers becomes even more desirable when a retired person gives up former status and financial reward.

Dear Ruth:

*I used to think that life in retirement would be a serene
and untroubled existence. However, during the past
three years in this condominium area I have seen as
much unrest and conflict among some of my neighbors as
I ever witnessed in the working world.*

*I don't believe that retirees should become uncon-
cerned or phlegmatic, but I am baffled when I
observe them getting into all kinds of petty fights over
trivial matters.*

*For example, three of my neighbors are actually not
speaking to three other neighbors in the building because
they cannot agree on who should run social affairs,
how much money should be collected or spent, how
and where various meetings should be held, etc.*

*Some of these people were in businesses or professions
before retirement, respected by colleagues and employers
or employees. Apparently they spent thirty or forty*

*years in some worthwhile capacity, then planned to
retire to a rewarding life in a healthful climate with
contemporaries with whom they had something in
common.*

*Instead of contributing constructively to their new
way of life, all they seem to do now is argue and
bicker among themselves. If this continues, won't it
increase the risk of high blood pressure and heart
attacks? And what causes this to happen to some people
once they retire?*

Concerned Charley

Dear Concerned Charley:
*You have described a distressing psychological reaction
to retirement "shock" which, unfortunately, is not
uncommon, particularly in retirees who held positions of
status before retirement.*

*The loss of respect and prestige is not easy to overcome,
especially if a retired person is unprepared to replace
the traumatic loss with other rewards.*

*What appears to be "trivia" to the objective onlooker
may loom large in the eyes of the person trying to find
new values in this unfamiliar environment. Therefore,
the organization of a social affair is as vital as a business
merger; the collection of dues is as urgent as the company
budget; the decorum of a meeting becomes as important
as the election of chairman of the board.*

*If your three neighbors are willing to destroy friend-
ship and goodwill in the process of finding themselves,
of course they are doing more harm than good,
both to themselves and others. Some retired people take
longer to evaluate their new environment in terms of
a positive and healthy attitude. No doubt there will be an
increase in accelerated pressure and heart conditions
if constant flare-ups are substituted for compromise and
understanding.*

*If you are truly concerned, perhaps you can influence
your neighbors to work together on some project which
might help those in the community less fortunate than
themselves.*

Do all people pull further apart as they grow older, or are there relationships that grow better with age? The letter that follows is all too rare, but there is evidence of people mellowing and improving when they relax alone together and really start to care. Watching couples walking hand in hand, riding bicycles, and romancing in retirement communities as if they were starting all over again (and some of them are *not* married) gives the observer pause for thought. In conducive surroundings, without strain, and with a vigorous attitude toward life in general, older people can breeze through the later stages with more joy and fulfillment than they ever realized earlier in life.

Dear Ruth:

In reading your column we notice that you get a lot of complaints from wives about husbands and husbands about wives. This is one letter that has no complaints! We are a couple in our sixties who retired at the same time from a life full of responsibility and concern for others. In the last two years we have thought only of each other for the first time since our children were born. It has been sheer delight to rediscover each other, to talk to each other, to walk with each other, and to love each other. We'd like to suggest to those squabbling couples who keep finding all kinds of faults to stop wasting time and start enjoying these wonderful years of getting older side by side.

Darby and Joan

Dear Darby and Joan:

Thank you for telling it the way it is with many retired couples who are finding this new stage a voyage of rediscovery.

CHAPTER III

SEX IS ONLY FOR THE YOUNG?

One of the most outdated myths about older people is that they are no longer interested or involved in sexual enjoyment. The frustrating notion was somehow perpetrated that romance and physical intimacy are prescribed only for the first few decades of life. No wonder some people who blindly believe this legend frantically try to do all their sexual living before they are "ripe" enough to truly appreciate it. Recent studies, including those of Masters and Johnson, have proved conclusively that there is no age limit to sexual responsiveness provided an individual is of sound mind and body. A healthy person of *any* age who finds a congenial partner in a pleasant atmosphere at the right time, who is not inhibited about age or anything else, will certainly be able to enjoy a gratifying relationship. There is no doubt that society and the media's constant stress on youth and its sexual prowess have

53

been instrumental in giving middle-aged and older persons a sexual inferiority complex. Many persons have found fear of failure, shame, and other mixed feelings about their own reactions inhibiting factors as they have grown older.

Strong emotional feelings and reactions toward members of the opposite sex are as evident in older people as they are in younger ones. Women can continue to be as jealous when they are married forty years as they are when they are married four. Here is a typical example.

Dear Ruth:

My husband has always been a loyal, devoted spouse with eyes for no other female than me. I was always proud of the way he paid undivided attention to me and never tried to flirt with other women at parties like some husbands.

We've been married a long time and I know my husband still cares for me. However, since we have retired, he keeps turning to look at the attractive women he sees and makes comments about their physical measurements. Do I have something to worry about, or is my husband just turning into a foolish old man?

Wife of Don Juan

Dear Wife:

It would seem to me that the time for concern about your "sexy" spouse should not be now.

Perhaps your husband did not have the time or opportunity to notice much about the opposite sex before retirement. Now that he is totally relaxed and does not have to contend with other pressures he is beginning to make up for lost time. This does not mean that he is likely to contemplate unfaithfulness or anything like that.

Your husband is simply responding as most of the normal, healthy male population, albeit at a slightly

*more advanced stage in his life. You should be glad
that he makes no attempt to hide how he feels,
which demonstrates his faith and appreciation of your
understanding. Certainly there cannot be much danger
in "looking." It is not necessary to possess a beautiful
work of art in order to enjoy gazing at it!*

*On the other hand, if your husband is trying to tell
you something, it might be worth your while to
listen. Have you given any real thought to your vital
statistics lately?*

When an older man is in good health but is aware
of declining sexual vigor, he frequently suffers from a
loss of self-esteem. Researchers indicate that inactivity
may be one of the causes of decline, blaming "nonuse
rather than abuse" as a cause of impotency. When a
married couple have a close relationship, this problem
need not develop into a neurosis, particularly since
professional consultation is readily available.

Dear Ruth:

*A recent article on sex research stated that sexual
vigor does not decrease in older people.*

*From personal experience, I can't agree. I am a man in
my early sixties in good health and happily married.
Our three children are adults and do not live at home.
We get along very well and have no serious problems
except for the fact that I am losing interest in sex.*

*I have not discussed this situation with my wife
because I don't want her to feel that I have stopped
loving her. I would like to know if it's possible for a man
to be less sexually active as he grows older and still
have a "normal" marital relationship.*

Troubled Husband

Dear Troubled:

Sex research does not get vital statistics from all older people. Although it is true that many men in good physical, mental, and emotional condition maintain sexual enthusiasm frequently into their seventies and eighties, there are other reasons for decreased activity in younger men. One of them is a fear of impotence rather than the actual condition.

If you have a close relationship with your wife, why can't you discuss this with her? She must be aware of the problem and probably wants to share it with you. Talking it out may bring you the assurance you seek, as well as cooperation from your wife.

On the other hand, it definitely is possible for some married couples to be content and secure in each other's love as they grow older with a decreased rate of sexual activity. However, if the situation continues to be troubling, it might be helpful for you to consult a sympathetic doctor (if you have one). Try to locate a clinic that is equipped to treat the sexual problems of married couples.

Many reputable sex clinics are affiliated with universities and hospitals. The local affiliate of Planned Parenthood should be able to refer you to a trained sex therapist.

In any case, don't give up. Remember, you may be getting older, but you don't have to get colder!

One of the realities that has to be faced by married couples is the loss of a spouse and the subsequent adjustment. The attitude of adult children, relatives, and friends when the remaining partner contemplates a new alliance can be very troubling to the widow or widower.

Dear Ruth:

My father is seventy-six years old and, though he has a mild heart condition, is "keeping company" with a woman of sixty-four whom he plans to marry. My sister and I are upset about this and are trying to discourage Father. We know nothing about the lady, but we think it's wrong for a man of his age and physical condition to undertake a second marriage. How can we make him understand that we are interested only in his welfare?

Concerned Son

Dear Concerned:

The fact that your father is seventy-six and has a mild heart condition is not enough reason for him to spend the rest of his life alone. If you are interested in his welfare, you will not hinder this marriage but welcome it. Since you and your sister have lives of your own, you should be glad that your father also wants one. You mention nothing about financial arrangements, so I assume that you will not need to contribute to the couple's support. However, even if such a contingency should develop, you should be prepared to add a little to your father's independence so that he need not become a burden. I would also suggest that you get to know the lady; you may find that you agree with your father. In any case, as knowledgeable adults of this generation, you must be aware that the need for a meaningful relationship between the sexes is as vital at seventy-six as it is at forty-six. If your father's heart should beat a little more rapidly in the years to come, it may be more helpful to his condition than any kind of medicine!

━━━━━━━━

The archaic attitude still prevails that a widow should observe a "proper" period of mourning, which includes isolation from normal companionship, especially that of members of the opposite sex.

> *Dear Ruth:*
>
> *One of our neighbors has been severely criticized for her open attitude in searching for a mate. Her second husband died less than a year ago. She started going out again a month after he passed away. Isn't there something wrong with a woman who acts in such an unfeeling way? In all other respects she is a very nice person, and goes out of her way to be helpful and friendly.*
>
> *Puzzled Neighbor*

> *Dear Puzzled:*
>
> *Since time immemorial lonely people have been searching for mates. It is only the mores of society that dictate the "proper" attitude!*
>
> *Your neighbor sounds like a rather unconventional but brave and realistic woman. She may prefer not to wear her bereavement on her sleeve; instead she is trying to cope in her own way. Certainly in this day and age, no one should tell anyone else what period of mourning should be observed. Since this was her second husband, it is also possible that she is not suffering such profound grief. In any case, if she's as nice a person as you describe, why not continue to appreciate her for her assets? You may be sure that the new friends she will acquire when she presents her next husband will be quite forgetful of the length of her mourning period.*

The story of the reluctant widower is not a new one, but occasionally—after succumbing to a second marriage—he is faced with a situation for which he is unprepared. The woman in this case also was not prepared to be merely a domestic replacement, but wanted as much from the second relationship as she was fortunate enough to experience in her first marriage. Some older people refuse to equate love, romance, and sex with "nonsense," despite the fact that they are far from being teen-agers.

Dear Ruth:

I hope you won't think me a foolish old man, because to me this problem is a disturbing one.

I was a widower for several years and resisted the thought of remarrying as long as I could for two reasons. The first one was that I was very devoted to my wife and felt it would be disloyal to her memory. The other reason was that I began to enjoy the new freedom of not having to answer to anyone but myself.

Recently I was introduced to an attractive divorcee twelve years younger than I am. Before I realized what was happening I was hooked! Although I am fond of my second wife, I now find myself in a situation which is making me unhappy as well as uncomfortable. My wife has some strange notions about a second marriage. Instead of settling down to a normal, peaceful routine, she constantly wants to go places and do things. Furthermore, she is not content with companionship but insists that I "romance" her as if we were a couple of teen-agers! How can I convince my wife that I am getting too old for this kind of nonsense?

Wistful Ex-Widower

Dear Wistful:

You certainly are not foolish in recognizing that you have a disturbing problem. Usually an individual who has a satisfactory first marriage tries to replace it as quickly as possible with a second marital union. Your expression in regard to "not having to answer to anyone" appears to indicate that perhaps you were not as blissfully wedded as you preferred to believe.

Apparently you were swept off your feet by a charming woman, but there is no reason to regret this bold step—if you really care for her. The difference in your ages might account for the difference in attitude to a certain extent—but not necessarily. You might have reacted to your first wife exactly the same way if she were alive. Perhaps your second wife's notions, second marriage or not, are not as peculiar as you think. You should be grateful to her for not encouraging you to sink into a mental and physical rut. An excellent way to age rapidly is to stop going places and doing things. As for "romance," if you are a healthy, normal man it might be a very rewarding experience for you to revive that beautiful love-glow once again. Stop feeling "hooked" and start contributing to what could become a truly warm and delightful second relationship at this stage of your life.

Another area of sexual concern is the one in which disparity of age plays a large part. In one case, the man is twenty years older than his proposed bride; in the other, the woman is eight years older than the proposed groom. Although the latter occurs far less frequently, it poses a serious problem for a courageous woman. If the straitjacket of convention should eventually loosen a few of its strings, the older woman-younger man marriage might be a solution to the uneven ratio of widows to widowers.

Dear Ruth:

I am a widower, seventy years old, and am planning to marry a woman twenty years younger than I am. She is very peppy, energetic, and youthful, and some-

times I get concerned about whether I will be capable of
sexual performance with such a woman. I am in good
health, play golf, swim, dance, and have young ideas.
Do I have reason to be concerned, and is there
something I can do to insure a successful marriage?

Worried William

Dear Worried:

A long time ago some Victorian myth was incorporated
into our stereotypes about sex and older people, but
most people over sixty today know better than that!
Modern medical authorities have reassured older people
that—provided they keep themselves fit and vigorous—
they will be able to have an active sex life as long
as they desire. If your description is accurate, you
definitely have nothing to be concerned about. Why
not talk to your family doctor? With a healthy body
and your attitude, you have already done much to insure
a successful marriage.

Dear Ruth:

I am a woman in her late fifties who has just been
proposed to by a bachelor who is eight
years younger. Although I care for him and think we
could have a good life together, I am afraid to consider
his proposal seriously. For one thing, I am concerned
about what my relatives and friends will say. For
another, I am worried that he will grow tired of an
older woman in a few years. Right now we have many
interests in common and are very compatible.

J.M.

Dear J.M.:

It is ludicrous that convention frowns on the older
woman-younger man union, but smiles on the opposite.
Nevertheless, I think you should consider this bachelor's
marriage proposal very seriously. Apparently he admires
and cares for you or he wouldn't have offered to give
up his freedom at this point. Your relatives and friends

61

*are not the ones who have to live without affection
and companionship . . . so it's not any of their business.*

*As far as a man's tiring of an older woman in a few
years, this sort of thing could also happen if the reverse
were true. Besides, I'd like to point out that the
desirability of older women to younger men is definitely
not a legend. In the year 1745 Benjamin Franklin
wrote, "Advice to a Young Man," which is as apropos
today as it was then. The following is a partial quote
from the eight reasons he gives for preferring older
women:*

*"Because as they have more knowledge of the world
and their Minds are better stor'd with observations, their
Conversation is more improving and more lastingly
agreable. . . . Because when Women cease to be handsome, they study to be good. They learn to do a
one thousand Services small and great, and are the most
tender and useful of all Friends when you are sick.
Thus they continue amiable. . . . Because there is no
hazard of Children, which irregularly produced may be
attended with much Inconvenience. . . ."*

No commentary intended to dispel the myth that
older people have lost their interest in sex would be
complete without reflections from the people themselves. In our class rap sessions on sexuality and aging,
several of the participants contributed significant
information.

Margaret—a trim, well-groomed woman in her
fifties—was outspoken about the newfound sexual
compatibility within her marriage: "Since I have
stopped worrying about pregnancy, John and I have a
much better sex life. Of course we took all sorts

of precautions for years, but that's one stage of life I'm very happy is over."

A stocky, balding man about sixty added his experience of the last few years: "Maybe it's because we have complete privacy for the first time in many years that Janet and I can express ourselves as freely as we did when we were first married...before the children came."

Married couples in the group were almost unanimous in agreeing that one of the advantages of growing older in a "good" marriage was the freedom to give more pleasure to each other. They spoke enthusiastically of getting dressed up to go out to dinner together, going shopping together, entertaining friends, exploring new areas of the city and state, planning family visits and trips to just "nowhere."

The warmth and rapport obviously had not suffered from several decades of matrimony. Shared experiences and problems had brought many couples closer together, so that, contrary to the cynic's viewpoint, marriage got better as they got older.

We don't often hear about these happy couples because, unfortunately, good marriages don't make news as separations and divorces do.

CHAPTER IV

LEISURE IS NOT FOR EVERYBODY

Most people look forward to using their leisure time in ways which will bring pleasure and relaxation. This is perfectly reasonable and understandable when they work five or six days a week for seven or eight hours each day. It is then that a hobby, a sport, or other recreational activity becomes "the pause that refreshes" both mind and body. No matter how much the average person enjoys his work, he looks forward to holidays and vacations. Subconsciously he feels that he has earned the right to use his leisure time as he sees fit, and he tries to crowd as much as possible into those hours until the next free time materializes.

Try asking any young person working hard at a time-consuming job or career whether he would like to have more leisure; you know the usual answer. If you were to hint at the idea that he might find additional leisure time boring and even undesirable, he would think you were putting him on. Yet that same young person, thirty or more years later, will be faced with just such a situation. Why?

For one thing, training is provided in many different areas for the young, but there are no courses in preparation for leisure. This is something that is supposed to come about naturally. And as long as there are just a *few* leisure hours, it works.

As children and young adults we became interested in all kinds of activities and pastimes. Some of them appealed to us more than others, or we showed more ability in some areas, so we pursued them more avidly, perhaps becoming proficient in one of them. If we were good at tennis, we probably spent much of our free time on the tennis courts. If we liked water sports, we went to the beach. If we enjoyed art, we went to a museum. If we liked to read, we browsed in the library. If we had a boat, we went sailing. If we liked eating outdoors, we called the gang and had a picnic in the park.

Leisure was fun. It provided a chance to get away from work, duties, chores, obligations, and was all the more precious because there was a limited time in which to enjoy it. This was also true if we liked our work and looked forward to Monday morning, mostly because of the difference between the two lifestyles.

A few decades later we are faced with the prospect of all the leisure we can handle. Either we decide to chuck it all and retire voluntarily, or our employers let us know the time has come. We may have tried to avoid this day for as long as possible. . .or we may have looked forward to it. In any case, what are we going to do with all this leisure? Are we going to play tennis, go swimming, attend museums and libraries, go sailing or picnicking? Will we still want to do these things, or will we want to try something new?

As a resident of a retirement community, I have observed what happens to people in their fifties and sixties who have headed into a life of idyllic leisure. The popular stereotype of the game-playing, pool-sitting, constantly socializing retiree holds true for a number of people in the first year or two of adjustment to unplanned leisure. This period can be likened to a honeymoon in which the newly wedded couple float blissfully in a glow of enchantment. The tensions of the working years seem to roll off their shoulders almost magically, and the golden years of a never ending vacation stretch indefinitely into the future.

For some it may take months, for others it may take years, but sooner or later the "honeymooners" settle down to face the necessity of a new life-style. From what I have seen, they generally fall into one of three major groups. The largest group engages with frenzied fervor in all kinds of unrelated meaningless activities—anything which will make the time go more quickly. Spending an evening playing bingo in the clubhouse or going to dinner with friends at a new restaurant becomes a highlight. The visit of married children and their families is planned for as if royalty were expected.

At the other extreme are those who prefer to quietly disengage themselves from most activities. They tend to their shopping and housekeeping chores, pick up the morning mail, visit a neighbor nearby, read the newspaper, and watch television. This routine may be varied with separate card games for the women and men.

Somewhere between these groups is a much smaller one that is involved in organizational and charity projects, volunteer hospital and community drives, church activities, and political campaigns. In this group are the people who were meaningfully involved in their preretirement positions and are seeking to rebuild similar, meaningful structures. They come the closest to having discovered that "leisure is not for everybody."

The *American Heritage Dictionary* defines leisure as "freedom from time-consuming duties, responsibilities and activities." The two largest groups in retirement have achieved this "freedom" but how truly free are they? When there are no duties, responsibilities, or activities to "consume" the time, what is left for people who may spend as many as twenty or twenty-five years in a leisure-oriented society?

It is my contention that, although older persons have the right to choose their personal life-style for the remainder of their years, the ones who choose to make the *most* of it rather than the *least* provide a valid and significant contribution not only to society but to themselves. However, many older people are strongly influenced by the unwritten rule of convention that leisure has been rightfully earned after the labors of a lifetime. It is not easy to admit that frequently leisure is *not* all that desirable and, in fact, may become, with the advent of the years, a dull, repetitious routine of meaningless meandering.

When it was necessary for me as a columnist to be as reassuring as possible to readers seeking answers to the problems of leisure, I was occasionally guilty of agreeing that withdrawal or meaningless activity would not be harmful in the overall picture of retirement. I have since had good reason to change my mind.

68

I have discovered that the most youthful, interesting, and rewarding people I know in retirement are those who are not concentrating chiefly on themselves. Don't get me wrong—I am not referring only to altruistic do-gooders. I am talking about those older people who have stretched the definition of "leisure" to include involvement, participation, and contribution in their broadest ramifications.

The first year that my husband and I became voluntary residents of the Greenbrier complex in Century Village was a term of exploration of the land of leisure for us. As a retired educator, Len had the motivation and expertise to organize a semistructured experiment in group living. We decided to call it "Greenbrier College," and by subtle solicitation and encouragement we were able to draw together some twenty volunteer "instructors." These were neighbors who had particular skills or abilities in various fields and who could be persuaded to teach a "course" to Greenbrier residents for a six- to eight-week "semester." The eager anticipation with which a hundred or more men and women lined up to enroll for courses during registration week made us realize that leisure most definitely is *not* for everybody. Again the groups divided themselves into three broad categories. The largest milled about, noisily asking questions, breaking out of the registration lines, and contributing little to the scene at hand. Another group stood on the sidelines—quiet, withdrawn, silently critical, and also not contributing much.

Those in the smallest group were the volunteer teachers and organizers, prepared to give their leisure time fully and freely, accepting "time-consuming duties, responsibilities and activities" (see dictionary definition) with remarkable interest and goodwill.

As I write this, Greenbrier College is still in existence, offering two semesters every winter. New courses and teachers are added each semester, and the students continue to enroll. They receive no academic credit, but each is presented a diploma. The success of this pseudo "college" experiment is undeniable proof that for many retirees *leisure is not enough*, when it does not lead to gratification or achievement of some kind.

You may ask, "What if a Greenbrier College is not available where I live and I have also just discovered that a lifetime of leisure is not enough? What else is there?" Since one of the purposes of this chapter is to provide practical suggestions for the persons who want more out of life as they get older, I shall conclude with some that have been tried and found worthwhile.

An invaluable asset before you start is your *attitude*. If you are determined to make leisure the most exciting and meaningful *activity* of your whole life, you have won half the battle. You have to decide now that you have a *purpose* and *reason* for living, just as you had in your first decades of life. A recent study made by a leading life insurance company showed that scientists rank first among those who live to an advanced old age, then clergymen and educators. Obviously the reason is that scientists and educators are constantly using their minds to search for answers, and clergymen are constantly using their faith and dedication to help others.

Whatever you do, don't be *idle*. There is a big difference between relaxing and being idle. Relaxing is what you appreciate doing after you have accomplished something. Being idle becomes being miserable because you have nothing to do. Physical health requires physical activity, and mental health necessitates mental activity. A sensible use of leisure time involves combining these two areas in a flexible but loosely organized arrangement. Most women find the use of leisure far less of a problem than men when they retire. A wife, particularly, continues to clean, cook, shop, schedule social and other engagements, and look after her husband and herself with very little break in her routine. In many cases new responsibilities are added because now her spouse requires more attention than before. If she is a widow she faces the problem of loneliness, but still maintains a home and continues her chores, such as they are.

Most men, having been dependent on the status and routine of their work or professional careers, have a greater adjustment to make to a day that now appears to have small purpose or meaning. No alarm reminds them every morning that they are needed somewhere outside their home, and that other people are waiting for them. At first being able to ignore the alarm clock comes as a relief. Sometimes this placid feeling lasts for months or even years. Eventually, however, most retirees are faced with the haunting question: "Is this *all* there is?"

So you start a search for "something else." If you had a special interest or hobby when you were younger, you might be able to renew it. Since you are now able to devote more time and energy to it, you are that much ahead. You might even get so good that you can turn your hobby into a part-time business or a full-time career. But you may not want to go that far; you just want something to "pass the time" pleasantly.

71

Usually such hobby does not bring the same feeling of purpose and accomplishment as one that provides a challenge.

"How do I find a hobby that's a challenge?" you ask. Think of something you have always wanted to do but were too scared, too lazy, or too busy to try. Go to your local library and do some reading and research on the subject. Then go out and get materials and get started. Or if there is a course on the subject at the local high school or adult education center, take it. Before long you will have an exciting project you will want to work on every day. You will also discover other people who have the same or a similar hobby, and you will never lack for a conversational topic of mutual interest. If there is a by-product of your interest or hobby, it will provide you and others with pleasure. If you choose to paint you may not become the greatest artist in America, but you can experience the thrill of being able to hang your own pictures on the wall or of giving a hand-painted vase of your own creation to a friend.

If you are not hobby-oriented, no matter what the size of the community in which you live you are needed. Get in touch with the organizations that can make use of your experience, your background, and yes—your *age*. An older person has much to offer the community that a younger person hasn't the time, interest, or patience for. The school system may welcome your assistance with teachers, with children, with directing traffic, in the lunchroom or on the playground. Palm Beach County has a remedial reading program in which volunteers are trained in a six-week program to help youngsters raise their reading level. The reaction of a child to an older person who helps on a one-to-one basis may well bring once-in-a-lifetime gratification. There are day-care centers where supervision is needed for the small children of working mothers. Children in underprivileged areas can benefit tremendously when adults take them on trips to a zoo, museum, or planetarium. Schools often appreciate older persons who are willing to speak on their travels, hobbies, or experience. A retired photographer I met took on the project of teaching sixth graders the art of taking and developing their own pictures. When he told me about it he added, "This is the most challenging job I've ever had."

Your town has Boy Scout and Girl Scout troops and Big Brother organizations that need adult leaders. Political and charitable organizations welcome volunteer workers with open arms. Most hospitals can use volunteer help. The Red Cross and Cancer and Heart Funds are constantly looking for workers. The Chamber of Commerce, Community Chest, and Mental Health Services may well be able to use your assistance. Certainly your church will have areas in which your services are vitally needed. Our town has an organization known as "Helping Hands" that reaches everywhere into the community, using volunteers to give help wherever it is needed. The American Association of Retired Persons is a national organization with chapters in over six hundred cities where people from every walk of life find common interests and goals.

One retired citizen, an energetic woman with unusual musical ability, organized talented volunteers to entertain in nursing homes, hospitals, and schools; they also raise funds for charitable organizations by putting on musical and dramatic programs. The Ida Alter Variety Performers of West Palm Beach, Florida, have become so popular that they have been paid for their performances, but have elected to turn the proceeds over to the Heart, Cancer, and Multiple Sclerosis funds. One of the most rewarding experiences Len and I have had since retirement was being part of the Ida Alter troupe.

Any activity which requires group participation is stimulating, especially if it has a purpose. The purpose may be service to others or enrichment of one's own life-style, but it usually does not survive long without a fundamental meaning or challenge. Many retirees are going back to school, either to take a course in an area they never had time to explore, to continue an education that they never completed, or to receive a degree just to see if they can do it.

If you do no more than keep informed of the latest developments in today's world you will feel better qualified to raise your voice against social injustices and not feel you have to take a back seat because you are "too old." Not letting yourself fall behind the times is a marvelous antidote to mental and spiritual deterioration. Don't hesitate to write a letter to an editor or make a speech at a club meeting if you are convinced that your community will benefit from it. You have perceptions and insights now that you never had when you were young, and they may well be listened to if you have the gumption to voice them . . . and can do so effectively.

If hobbies, volunteer service organizations, continuing education, or community projects have no appeal for you, you may be motivated by a paying job. If you have received a salary most of your life, you may still feel the need for financial recognition of your worth. I would not play down the feeling of satisfaction this may bring—or the fact that it may also contribute a welcome addition to a limited budget.

In some areas employers are not sufficiently educated concerning the potential of older citizens and it may not be easy to find suitable work. Many people over sixty are physically fit, mentally alert, spiritually compatible, and a heck of a lot more responsible than a number of younger employees.

You may have to "create" a job where one is not in open evidence. You might offer to work on a voluntary basis for a specified time until the worth of your service is recognized and compensated. You might investigate if your community has an employment service geared to the needs of older people who want jobs; if one does not exist, perhaps you can get one started with other people who feel as you do.

"Sixty-five" is just an arbitrary number selected as a dividing line by Social Security authorities. If you are convinced, as I am, that retirement can mean *refirement* rather than retreat, there will be no stopping you. Again, do not neglect your health, because you cannot accomplish much when you are not well. If you are physically fit, you can do anything you want to at this stage of the game.

Perhaps this chapter sounds as if I am advocating a program of "all work and no play" for retired persons. I hasten to say that I am very much in favor of periods that have no other purpose than providing fun and relaxation. Just as when I was younger, I appreciate the games, picnics, and parties more because they are a contrast, not mere routine. I never want to get to that point in retirement when, as the unhappy man said, "Every day is like Sunday." How many years can healthy persons remain healthy if, from Monday to Saturday, all they have is Sunday?

If your idea of heaven has always been limitless leisure, it might be helpful to recall the experience of one of Mark Twain's characters. When Captain Eli Stormfield went to the Hereafter he found that, while sitting on a cloud bank, only three things happened. His halo became awfully heavy. He could not handle his wings. He could play only one tiresome tune on a harp that kept getting rusty.

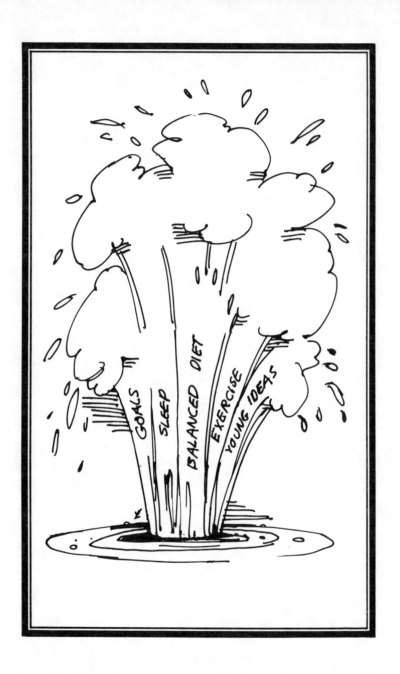

CHAPTER V

DO I HAVE TO GET SENILE?

During one of our rap sessions on "getting older and better" we discussed the unlimited potential of the lifespan in the next few decades. One of the participants was visibly troubled about the fact that scientists are trying to discover how to make people live longer. "Who wants to live longer?" he finally burst out. "Everyone knows you get senile if you live long enough."

This impression was shared by several persons in the group. After some discussion, we decided that those who felt this way had based their reactions on their knowledge of elderly people in mental hospitals, nursing homes, and other institutions. They were talking about *sick* people and equating mental and physical illness with aging. But how about all those older persons whose minds are alert and creative and whose bodies, though they may have slowed down, are still useful and well-preserved? Are these just the lucky ones? Or do most people who live long enough *have* to get senile?

Although some doctors still believe that physical deterioration in the brain causes senility, most social gerontologists and psychologists agree that the physically and mentally healthy older person need *never* demonstrate any symptoms of senility. In addition, recent scientific observations indicate that, contrary to general belief, human beings have an inborn potential to live a hundred years or more, and that even if they had short-lived parents, they can live up to this potential with relatively little effort.

Is there a secret formula which will accomplish this so-called "miracle" of aging? If we believe the biblical stories that Noah lived to be five hundred, Lamech seven hundred and seventy-seven, and Methuselah nine hundred and sixty-nine years old, then there must be a secret formula. If not, we must find something that will work for ordinary human beings like you and me.

Granted, the increased life expectancy of the average American in the course of this century has been due largely to medication and therapy used in treating certain diseases. There are now living in the United States over five thousand persons who are one hundred years old or older. You may nourish a wistful desire to be part of such a group but, like my cynical student, fear what this will bring with it. You may also wonder what these people are doing to make them live so long and still be able to function successfully.

Research studies conducted in recent years in the more primitive areas of the world have come up with results that are not only fascinating but should give us food for serious thought. There are a number of villages in southern Ecuador and elsewhere where groups of people not only are living well beyond the century mark but also are reputed to retain their faculties and health to a remarkable extent.

If we are able to apply to our own lives some of the findings of the medical and scientific investigating teams, we too should benefit from them. Although we cannot realistically duplicate their environmental factors we certainly can modify dietary and psychological factors involved in aging. The most impressive part of the reports about these communities is the *attitude* demonstrated toward their oldest residents. Centenarians are more than merely tolerated. They are expected to live useful and dignified lives—and that is exactly what they do. Each one has a job or responsibility in the community, according to his or her *ability*. Despite what we consider advanced age, many of them are clear-eyed, move briskly, do their own housework, cooking, and other chores, and require no more assistance than some of the younger residents. Interviewers noted that many of these people were outgoing, sociable, and displayed a sense of humor that might well be envied by individuals half their age. Third and fourth marriages were commonplace among men and women past their ninth and tenth decades. Age was something to *boast* about. What a contrast to Western society where older people are intimidated, fearful, and in some cases pressured into concealing their birthdays!

Another noteworthy fact about these Ecuadorians' health is that they seldom suffer from cancer, heart disease, and diabetes, and yet in larger cities and towns these afflictions are found. It was reported that their

81

diet is rather monotonous and austere, because for the most part they are poor people. We should be aware that the causes of earlier deaths among wealthy people, especially those who dine on rich food, are heart ailments and other diseases related to unhealthy dietary factors.

Another story has it that if you really desire to live long, you must choose two sets of long-lived grandparents. This, however, is not always conclusive. It is apparent that longevity seems to run in some families, whether of Ecuadorian or American background. Therefore it is natural that studies of human longevity will show a positive relationship between the longevity of grandparents, parents, and children. Most of these longevity studies completely omit the important effects of environment and controllable factors on longevity. In recent studies where investigators started examining more closely the environmental factors in the lives of people who lived to an advanced age with relatively few signs of deterioration, the specific circumstances and attitudes or those examined were found to be vitally important.

Almost half a century ago Walter Pitkin escalated to best selling fame with his book, *Life Begins at Forty.* People were willing and eager to accept this declaration, even though many of them kept their fingers crossed. Today, some five decades later, we are able to make another statement—with fingers no longer crossed. "Life begins at fifty - sixty - seventy - or whenever you want it to." Sweeping as this may sound, the implication behind it is what matters most.

You are *not* going to become senile if you are convinced that you *won't*. The contrary is much more probable, because then you will allow yourself to slump into the very mannerisms and characteristics you fear. When you *think* negatively, you *act* negatively. A fragment of conversation I overheard one afternoon between two men in a parking lot went something like this:

"Hello, Tom. How've you been?"

"Oh, so-so, Sam. What can you expect from old codgers our age?"

I turned to look at the last speaker who perhaps was in his early sixties. His friend, about the same age, wore a natty sport jacket over a trim, athletic body and flashed a broad, white-toothed smile from a tanned countenance. If I had been Sam, I would certainly have resented being placed in the same category as Tom!

Unfortunately, some people still tell themselves that life is practially over because they are sixty-five or seventy. Their thoughts and conversation center around their physical symptons and illnesses. They waste valuable time and energy that they could spend improving their minds and bodies. Of course it is true that one of the threats to an older person's self-image is the negative attitude of society in general, but if he allows this to influence his own thinking it will only hasten the very symptoms he dreads.

Many television programs today promote a negative image of aging. In a recent poll conducted by a national magazine readers were asked to check three words from a list of twelve "that you feel most accurately describe the way people over sixty are generally depicted on major TV shows." Here are the percentages of the total vote that each word got:

Ridiculous	- 38%
Decrepit	- 26%
Childish	- 25%
Mature	- 24%
Cranky	- 23%
Passé	- 22%
Dignified	- 17%
Wise	- 15%
Lively	- 13%
Petulant	- 12%
Moody	- 10%
With-it	- 9%

Inasmuch as a large proportion of TV viewers are supposedly people over sixty, I am surprised that they sit back and continue to accept the emphasis on aging stereotypes. Is there any reason why TV producers and writers in our enlightened century should be permitted to present unfair and exaggerated images of older people any more than of other age groups?

Is there anything *you* can do about it? You bet your boots there is! Bombard those TV stations with strong letters of protest; don't just switch to another channel— or worse yet, "grin and bear it." Don't continue to buy products whose commercials downgrade older people; boycott them consistently and let the producers know *why*. Older people comprise an important proportion of the consumer population. It makes sense for the informed TV program planners to include positive images of this group, but they will do so only if they are convinced that someone out there really cares.

If you indulge in feeling sorry for yourself, before long you are going to *look* sorry. Avoid the kind of "friends" who try to depress you by telling you how awful it is to get older. Depression is one of the signs of the approach of senility, but if you are busy setting goals every day of your life you won't have the time to be depressed. Mortimer Collins tells us that "the true way to render age vigorous is to prolong the youth of the mind."

The New York State Joint Legislative Committee on Aging Problems drew up a checklist some years ago which indicated you are not old unless—

> *You feel old.*
> *You feel you have learned all you need to learn.*
> *You find yourself saying, "I'm too old for that."*
> *You feel that tomorrow holds no promise.*
> *You find no amusement in youths' fun, and their banter irks you.*
> *You would rather talk than listen.*
> *You long for the good old days because you're sure they were the best.*
> *You won't help your neighbors, friends, or community.*
> *You have no plans for tomorrow.*
> *You would rather win an argument than appear to be wrong.*

What are some of the environmental factors we can control to retard the quality and quantity of growing older?

For one, with easier methods of transportation, we can change the climate to suit our physical and psychological needs. For another, with all the available knowledge on balanced diet and nutrition we can choose foods which will keep us from gaining excess weight or suffering from malnutrition. We know that the proper exercise in moderate amounts will help to keep us firm and shapely. We realize that the little pillows of flab add nothing to our appearance and also detract from our health and vigor. We understand that we need some rest every day and restful activities, but that too much rest and napping is useless. Without undue concern for our physical condition, we will have regular medical checkups as a precautionary measure, including optical and dental examinations. We also take special measures to avoid accidents.

We are aware that a number of changes take place as we get older so we take them in our stride because we know that, though they may slow us down a little, they don't have to disable or disfigure us in any way. For example, we may have to wear glasses, but since glasses are quite fashionable now whether we are twenty or eighty, what difference does it make other than that they are an aid to better vision? (And young women have taken to wearing "granny" glasses because they look so "cute.")

Maintenance of physical, mental, and emotional health is pretty much the same for an older person as for anyone else. Knowing that we need to take an extra measure of precaution is not a problem once it becomes a simple conditioned reflex. It's really a matter of common sense. In the next chapter I will discuss practical ways to eat, rest, sleep, and exercise to derive the most benefit from our later decades. Good health, in and out of retirement, will add years to our life and life to our years. Above all, it will help us to respond to the question, "Do we have to get senile?" with an emphatic, "We most certainly do *not!*"

CHAPTER VI

ANTI-AGING
HEALTH HABITS

Do people with poor health habits live to a ripe old age? Some do. My husband has an uncle in his eighties who does everything contrary to the promotion of sound health and longevity. He has never married, smokes two packs of cigarettes a day, eats most of his meals in restaurants, goes out in all kinds of weather, gets up early and goes to bed late, and sees a doctor only if he is dragged there by a solicitous niece or nephew. I personally know of only one of his habits that is noteworthy. He continues to walk several miles a day as he did for more than forty years on his job as a mailman. (In those days the United States postal service did not provide delivery vehicles.) However—and I say this with the knowledge that Uncle Ralph will never bother to read this book—he is one of the unhappiest oldsters I have ever known. He lives a lonely, empty, unfulfilled existence.

Does this prove that one can do (almost) everything wrong and live a long life? I don't know, but I prefer to believe that Uncle Ralph and others like him are exceptions. I forgot to mention that Uncle Ralph is a grouchy, irritable person who has few friends and fewer dutiful relatives. My money is on people like those about which a group of Soviet gerontologists reported some years ago. According to the report their mountain climate, sparse diet, and daily exercise all contributed to a healthy life-span well over the century mark. Furthermore, these people unfailingly manifested a cheerful, positive attitude about themselves and their roles in the life of the community. In examining the pictures of some of these centenarians I noted that there were no more wrinkles on their faces than I have observed on some seventy-year-olds—and far more pleasant facial expressions.

Since the human body is being continually rebuilt, new parts have to replace the old, worn-out ones. The food we eat plays an essential role in this process. Therefore a well-balanced diet provides the body with the raw materials it needs for the manufacture of replacements. Older persons who subsist on haphazard meals disregard the body needs of any age. When the proper foods are missing, the process of manufacture cannot go on efficiently. "We are what we eat" is an expression that is even more significant as we get older. Very few persons live long, healthy, happy lives on a poor diet. It has been proved conclusively that proper nutrition throughout the life cycle is one of the factors that help determine an individual's longevity. Diet is directly related to such ailments as atherosclerosis, hypertension, and diabetes. Fat people usually don't survive too long. (And while they are surviving they are not as happy about their rotundity as the fat man and lady caricatures indicate.)

Eating is a pleasant social custom, but an older person can eat less and still socialize just as pleasantly. A good way to eat less is to eat slowly. Try putting a little less on your plate and take longer to finish. Conversation with another person takes your mind off your food and causes you to eat more slowly. If you live alone, invite a friend to dine with you; you will both benefit by the meal and the company. Eating the right kinds of foods can be as pleasurable as eating the wrong kinds, although it does take a little more thought and preparation.

Sometimes an older person suddenly develops strange eating habits without apparent reason, causing his cook or eating companion considerable distress.

Dear Ruth:

My husband has recently developed a peculiar phobia about eating certain kinds of foods.

When he worked, he went out frequently for lunch and sometimes dinner (when working late) with some of the other men in the office. Since he has retired he insists on eating only bland foods cooked at home. He has an excellent stomach and can eat anything he wants, according to the doctor.

I am a good cook and don't mind preparing special foods if they are ordered for medical reasons. However, my husband's complex creates an uncomfortable situation because we cannot accept dinner invitations at our friends' homes nor can we go out to dine without humiliating results. What do you think has caused my husband's strange eating habits?

Puzzled Wife

Dear Puzzled:

If your husband has no genuine physical reason for this sudden aversion to "regular" foods, we can assume that there may be some underlying psychological cause. It is possible that the years of being forced to eat so many meals in different restaurants has caused a revulsion in your husband to out-of-home-prepared meals. His preference for bland food suggests that he might be experiencing some discomfort with foods that require cutting, chewing, and careful digestion.

Perhaps the thought of spicy or exotic foods evokes a subconscious fear of arousing spicy or exotic feelings erroneously associated with such foods. Sometimes, inwardly confused or insecure people tend to shy away from unfamiliar foods because this requires a confrontation with something for which they are unprepared.

If you are a good cook and your husband enjoys eating at home, he is also paying you a compliment. (Probably this is one compliment you would like to dispense with at this point.)

You may possibly be able to "cure" your husband's food phobia in one of several ways. Gradually and gently start spicing foods you prepare at home until he becomes accustomed to them. Consult a professional therapist. Or lay in a stock of strained baby foods!

———————

Perhaps my answer seems a bit facetious, but this is a rare example of a man growing wise in his nutritional habits as he became older. His wife's cooking made more sense after so many restaurant meals, especially since they agreed so well with his stomach.

Some people have the habit of eating much too much

food at one sitting. They may not be aware of this hazardous health habit because it has been a family custom for generations. Frequently they believe that the middle-aged paunch "runs in the family" when it is really nothing more than a consequence of eating styles.

It is important to realize that the body's capacity to burn fuel declines considerably with age. This means that as we get older more of the calories that we consume are converted into fat. Next to habitual overeating, the decline in our body's ability to burn fuel is the most significant cause of the weight increase. I was puzzled for some time to understand why, although I was eating no more than I had in my twenties, I was gradually putting on weight. When I learned that the answer was that my body's capacity to burn fuel was much less, I finally became aware that I would have to consume far less in order to maintain even the status quo. There is no doubt that if one wishes to maintain a trim appearance, good health, and a sense of well-being as he or she gets older, it will be necessary to exert a steady amount of discipline.

Just as some older people overeat, some undereat because they are worried about indigestion (or are following some food fad). Frequently loss of sleep, chronic irritability, and a feeling of lassitude stem from being undernourished. A large number of older persons suffer from malnutrition, which is really the lack of a balanced diet.

We should familiarize ourselves with the four groups of essential nutrients and make sure that they appear in our daily meals. They are easy to include in the average diet, but remembering to do so takes a little extra thought. The four groups are

Protein (milk, meat, fish, eggs, poultry)
Calcium and iron (milk, eggs, cheese, vegetables like spinach and cabbage)
B vitamins (unrefined cereals, bread, milk)
Vitamin C (citrus fruits, tomatoes, raw cabbage, peanuts)

If you eat most of your meals at home, try posting this or a similar list on a kitchen wall, and after a while you will find you have memorized it. It is not difficult to include all or most of theses nutrients even if you eat a number of meals out. Eating the right kind and amount of food pays off handsomely in health.

An eating problem that creates difficulties for some retired persons is indicated in the following letter:

Dear Ruth:

In the short period that we have been retired in this new area, my husband and I have put on so much weight that I am absolutely miserable. We realize this must be caused by all the cocktail and dinner parties we've been attending, but we don't want to offend the new people we've been meeting. We have to return these invitations with the same kind of hospitality, and I dread the results. Do you have any advice for a pair of recently retired

Chubbies

Dear Chubbies:

Frequently when retired people relocate, their new neighbors and friends wine and dine them in a flattering round of parties such as you describe. Although it is a warm gesture on their part, it can pose a real problem. Usually this is only temporary; however it certainly proves that it does not take long for middle-aged and older people to put on extra pounds, for the reason that they no longer burn calories as they used to. You can continue to accept and give invitations without dreading the consequences if you do the following.

Ask your host or hostess for a small glass of juice instead of a cocktail and make sure that it takes all evening to drink it. In other words, hold that glass politely so that you are still in the spirit of the party, but don't let it become empty until the end of the evening. When it comes to the solid foods, eat only half of every portion you are served. Skip all the desserts and, if fresh fruit is not served, treat yourself to a piece when you get home. Better still, eat that fruit before you go to a party or before you serve food yourself, and it will help to curb your appetite. If you continue to be aware of what is happening and take immediate steps to counteract it, you and your husband should be able to take off the undesirable poundage. Keeping it off may be a matter of watchful vigilance for the rest of your lives.

Another problem of vital importance is what kind and how much exercise is needed as a person gets older. Some people have never followed a regular program of exercise of any kind, because it required too much time and discipline, or interfered with occupational and social routines. They assuaged their consciences with a weekend game of golf, an occasional swim in the neighborhood pool, or a nightly walk around the block with the family dog. (I am referring to the average middle-aged man or woman, not the tennis champ, football star, or ice-skating queen in their twenties.) Although we all heard how necessary it was to keep our bodies fit with daily exercise, somehow we were too weary after eight hours at a desk and driving a car through nerve-wracking traffic to do much more than relax after supper with television and the newspaper. Although thinking and making decisions had filled us with fatigue and tension, it had used up only small amounts of glucose. It had not helped us to stay fit and energetic or to reduce emotional strains. Furthermore, it was easier to conceal the thickening waistline and expanding tummy under a larger jacket than to start an exhausting program at the gym. A few of us may have made some feeble attempts when there was a local fitness campaign at reduced rates, but it never lasted very long.

And so now here we are—retired—and maybe we are convinced that exercise might be beneficial. We have the time, but we don't know where to start. Perhaps we're *afraid*, even though we're in good health, because somewhere there is a small worry at the back of our minds: "Am I too old to start, if I've done little or no exercise before in my life?"

According to Dr. Josef P. Hrachovec, author of *Keeping Young and Living Longer*, experience shows that "adult, middle-aged and older people can recapture a high degree of physical fitness even after years of sedentary life or inactivity. But they need to do it gradually, and they need an exercise program that begins at their present level of physical fitness." The good doctor uses the word *recapture*...but what if we have nothing to recapture?

The clues to eventual body tone and fitness are a couple of adverbs—*gradually* and *persistently*. With gradual persistence and real motivation, the most inept individuals are able to achieve rewarding results, no matter what their age. However, since a number of heart specialists are still quite cautious about recommending certain kinds of exercise for older persons, it is always advisable to have a complete medical checkup before embarking on a new physical life-style.

In my own experience at starting a new kind of physical activity after fifty, the result has been all the more gratifying because it was unexpected. Being married to a top, all-around athlete who keeps himself in excellent condition through regular tennis, swimming, and other vigorous activities is enough to give an inferiority complex to any ordinary, non-athletic non-exerciser. Therefore the first time I heard the term "Hatha Yoga" I perceived a very faint ray of hope. I was encouraged at the first session I took in an adult education course when the instructor informed us he was past sixty-five! His account of progressing from an arthritic, poorly coordinated, fatigued specimen to the lean, energetic individual who could pass for twenty years younger was inspiring to the few men and women in the room my age. Although I had a full-time teaching position and taught several evenings a week, I stuck with Hatha Yoga for the next few years. I learned, as so many uninformed laymen before me, that it was not necessary to sit on a bed of nails or meditate for hours in one position. I also learned that the movements involved in Hatha Yoga when practiced faithfully every day resulted in improved circulation, body tone, posture, breathing, flexibility, and self-confidence.

Yet when I moved into our retirement community in southern Florida and tried to introduce to a group of men and women over the age of sixty-five what I had been taught, the first session did not evoke the almost spontaneous reaction it had in me. It was then that I hit upon the idea of "*Yogacizes*," a modification and adaptation of gentle, beneficial movements partially based on Hatha Yoga and simple exercise plus a relaxation period. For the past three years, every morning (except Sundays) under the shaded pavilion at Greenbrier I am surrounded by a dedicated group of "Yogacizers" in leotards and swimsuits. The student who has shown the most progress is a seventy-four-year-old retired attorney who never did an hour's exercise of any kind in his entire life. He has taken off twenty-two pounds, has a taunt waistline, and moves like a man half his age. Furthermore his sixty-eight-year-old spouse recently informed me that *all* of Bob's "ideas" are getting younger, and she is having a bit of a time keeping up with him!

Many an older person reports a renewed sense of well-being and energy after several months of any kind of steady exercise. Going in for strenuous sports as one gets older is considered dangerous and inadvisable by medical authorities. But they all seem to be pretty much in agreement that one of the best anti-aging habits a person can form is to adhere to daily exercise. Among the most frequently noted causes of coronary heart disease are too much rich food and too little physical activity. Sitting around and doing nothing as one gets older only hastens the aging of the mind and body.

It is true some people tend to find a program of daily prescribed exercise uninspiring and routinized. One way of overcoming this dislike is to work out with a group. If this is still not your cup of tea, you may enjoy walking several miles in the fresh air with or without a companion, or riding a bicycle along the winding paths of a park or area where there is not much traffic. A common sight in many retirement communities is the three-wheeler that has sprouted as a result of the quest for physical activity without undue strain.

Whether your choice is Yoga, walking, bicycling, swimming, or an assortment of these does not matter. What matters most is not to forget to *do it daily* for at least thirty minutes. With twenty-four hours in every day, certainly 2.12 percent is not too much to spend as insurance against debilitating old age.

Frequently older people become concerned about the need for vitamins in their diet. All the research I have done in this connection seems to agree that if they stick to a well balanced diet of unrefined foods it is likely they will have no need of vitamin supplements. However, my observation of the average American's eating preferences is that they tend toward a mixture of refined and unrefined foods. (Refined refers to the process which changes food's chemical content.) Because refined foods appear to taste better to many people, they are served frequently on social occasions.

Even when the vitamin content in food is good, there is no assurance that your body is utilizing it fully. Since massive doses of some vitamins have been reputed to be harmful in some cases, it makes sense not to dose yourself with them unless your doctor prescribes them. On the other hand it is my feeling that, unless you suffer from a specific vitamin deficiency, it is worthwhile to fortify the average diet with a carefully selected multi-vitamin. When I discussed this with my family doctor he agreed that it could do no harm. How much good it would do he was not prepared to say. All I know is that when I *don't* take my multi-vitamin for a period of a month or more as a test, I feel a definite decrease in pep and energy. So, even if this is only a psychological placebo, it is one investment I consider relatively small in the anti-aging market.

The following comment from one of my readers brings into focus still another area in the concern of people growing older and trying to grow better.

> *Dear Ruth:*
>
> *I constantly hear people my age (mid-sixties) talking about going home to take a "little nap," even though they just finished with nothing more strenuous than lunch or gin rummy. I find that taking naps only succeeds in making me sleepless at bedtime. Please discuss how much sleep and rest are really needed by most people as they grow older.*
>
>

Wide Awake
>

> *Dear Wide Awake:*
>
> *Taking a nap immediately after eating or any other sedentary activity would seem totally unwarranted unless recommended by a physician. Although some people require more rest than others, it is important to realize that too much rest may result in disturbing relaxation at bedtime. You certainly don't have to take a nap just because other people your age do! They may not have anything more interesting to do with their afternoons. If you do, and you feel good about it, don't stop!*

Somewhere I read, "The road to aging is never a superhighway to paradise; it is full of curves, bumps, and rough spots, but these can be smoothed over by driving at the proper speed."

As we grow older, it may be true that we should pay more attention to the preservation and recharging of our energies than we did when they were available in greater amounts. Nevertheless, the generalization that the faster we live the faster we must age is a gross overstatement. Frequently just the opposite is true. The more *slowly* some individuals live the faster they age. A person with many challenges and responsibilities, who does not take too much time out for sleep and play, may mellow into a satisfactory, healthy old age. Another may sleep ten hours a night and take frequent daytime naps and fade into a premature, apathetic decadence. When the demands on the mind and body are either too many or too few, the course of aging will not be smooth or agreeable.

How, then, can we determine our needs for such vital factors as rest, sleep, and energy as we grow older? What is just as important—how can we distinguish the difference between the gradual normal changes in aging and serious conditions of poor health?

If there is a feeling of constant discomfort or irritation it is possible that we are not adapting well to the gradual diminution of energy that can reasonably be expected. Some people accelerate the pace of aging unknowingly by disregarding such feelings rather than accepting them. Too many strenuous activities will punish the mind and body, just as the other extreme will. If we have been habitually active, it will require self-understanding to stop for brief periods of rest when we find we are pushing ourselves. However, if we continue to be tired and listless even when we are not doing much, it is probable that resting less and getting more involved in meaningful activity will do the trick, provided health problems have been ruled out. Don't be afraid of pleasant fatigue; it is as essential as hunger or thirst. It means that the body is giving notice it

101

is ready to stop for a while to refuel. Excessive weariness may be a sign of ill health, but normal tiredness will dissipate with proper relaxation.

Frequently people who have sleepless nights turn to sleeping pills and sedatives, but medical authorities warn that such measures should be resorted to only in extreme cases. Sometimes a pattern of poor sleep can be traced to an emotional disturbance, and only when the problem is resolved is the insomniac able to return to restful sleep.

Among some of the helpful measures to promote sleep are the following: Involve yourself in outdoor physical activity during the day; have your main meal at noon and a light meal early in the evening; reduce your fluid intake (no coffee, tea, or coke); use a firm mattress; listen to relaxing music or read a light novel before bedtime; don't keep yourself awake by the *fear* that you won't be able to go to sleep. If all else fails, sit on the rug (in a quiet room with a dim light) and do ten or fifteen minutes of gentle Yogacizes. Then stretch yourself to sleep.

I should like to conclude this chapter with some challenging revelations from Dr. Hans Selye, the world's leading authority on stress. This Viennese physician has a code of behavior which may be valuable for persons in their later years. He believes emphatically that "complete freedom from stress leads to death. Don't try to avoid stress—it's the very salt and spice of life. But do learn to master and use it." Dr. Selye does not accept the notion that taking it easy is the way to a longer and heathier life—with good reason. In his scientific experiments with animals, he has been able to prove that abnormal strain will cause heart attacks, ulcers, and allergies. Abnormal or excessive stress is known as "distress"; compatible and useful stress is called "eustress." When eustress is correctly handled it provides a reason for living, especially for older people. They can't avoid stress, but if it's turned into eustress (such as finding an area in which they can succeed) it may mean the difference between fading away or igniting a new spark. "Of course," Dr. Selye continues, "some of us are turtles and some are racehorses. Force a turtle to run like a racehorse and you'll kill him. Force a racehorse to stand in his stall all day long and you'll kill him, too."

So, here's to all the racehorses *and* the turtles. Whatever you do, do it at your own pace—but *don't* stand still!

CHAPTER VII

WILL I HAVE ENOUGH?

Fear that pensions, social security, insurance, and savings will not provide an adequate income have delayed the retirement of some persons beyond their original plans. Sometimes an individual who was not mentally or emotionally prepared for a changed financial status responds like the spouse in the following letter.

Dear Ruth:

What would cause a kind, generous husband to turn into a grouchy, petty "skinflint" in retirement?

In all our married life, my husband never questioned or complained about any household or other expenditures. As a matter of fact, he took pride in the realization that I always managed to keep our home, our children, and ourselves tastefully but not extravagantly adorned.

Since we have retired, he has become obsessed with every penny I spend, even though our income is very adequate to maintain a decent standard of living.

He insists there is no need to replace shoes or clothing no matter how shabby they become. He walks around in sloppy shirts and baggy pants that are disgraceful relics. When I pointed out that our thirty-five-year-old couch needed recovering, he claimed there was at least another twenty years' wear in it!

He has limited our entertaining menu to cookies and lemonade or tea. If I try to serve our guests anything more, he becomes furious. When I try to reason with him, he answers that retired people are not supposed to live like people who are working.

How can I help my husband return to the generous man he was before retirement?

Skinflint's Wife

Dear Skinflint's Wife:

It is not unusual for hidden fears or resentments to rise to the surface when a person retires to an inactive or frustrating existence.

Apparently the pride and security your husband felt as the head of the household have vanished. Even though you mention a "very adequate" income, your husband himself feels less than adequate.

He is beset by the fear that the money may give out, simply because he is no longer earning it every day as he used to. Money may always have been his security blanket, and now he cannot bear to feel it being pulled off his shoulders by an "extravagant" wife. Your expenditures may now be erroneously interpreted by your spouse as selfish and frivolous gestures.

Your husband is not alone in the mistaken archaic belief that older people have far fewer economic needs than when they were young. If he was the kind of man you describe before retirement, it is unlikely that he feels any real joy or pride at seeing his home, his wife, or himself looking worn and neglected. This reaction may be only an outer symptom of a much deeper problem.

Your husband can use understanding and reassurance from you until he manages to overcome this concern.

You might try sympathizing with him. Let him know
that you are able and willing to economize whenever it
is necessary. You might even take a part-time job so that
you will have "pin money" for those extras.

It is also important for your husband to discover
some absorbing activity or interest that will keep his
mind off his worries—and himself. At this time of life,
it is no longer that urgent to save for a rainy day,
especially in your secure economic situation.

It may be a wise and happy practice to spend a little
on a sunny day—while you are both still able to enjoy it!

You can never be positive how much money you will
need during retirement years. Much depends, of course,
on your state of health, standard of living, and the
overall financial conditions in the country and world
at the time. As an average middle-class American,
however, you can generally count on a number of
positive factors. You will not have to support adult
children (in most cases). Your own living expenses will
decrease, especially if you relocate in a rural area or
the South, where housing, food, and clothing expenses
are generally lower. You no longer need to live in a
large house or a costly neighborhood. You can get
by with a smaller car and a smaller backyard. You
will enjoy entertaining on a less lavish scale and
belonging to clubs that do not charge exorbitant dues.
The expenses involved in transportation to and from
your place of employment, the cost of work lunches,
the need for business clothes, conventions, equipment,
etc., will stop with retirement. Federal and state income

taxes generally will be reduced. Real estate and personal taxes may be reduced if you move into a lower tax-assessment community. If you now have a mortgage it will probably be paid off before you reach retirement age.

There are other ways to cut down on expenses too. Frequently a working wife does not have time to be economical. She may have to pick up frozen or easily prepared foods on the way home from work. Some retirees enjoy raising their own vegetables, which helps reduce food costs. There is also more time to perform odd jobs and repairs around the house instead of hiring someone to do them. And women who formerly paid a seamstress to make alterations in their clothing may now enjoy the challenge of doing their own.

For most people the years between thirty-five and sixty-five are the ones in which earning power is at its highest. Intelligent and farsighted planning in the forties and fifties will help to solidify a workable income for the future, as well as instill a certain amount of confidence. Many authorities on retirement planning suggest drawing up a statement of net worth—what one owns and the form in which it exists, together with what is owed, the nature of obligations, and the surplus that exists between the two. Knowing where one stands is an aid to wise planning in reaching a level of economic security in retirement.

Some people become upset when faced with the necessity of planning a strict budget. It is better to simply map out a flexible outline of the way in which they intend to allocate their approximate income. What may work for some retirees will not work for all—it is an individual matter—but there is general knowledge that is useful for everyone.

People living on a fixed income are always affected by the rising cost of living known as inflation. Frequently a couple will skimp and save throughout their working lifetime, going without many things in order to save for later. But savings are fixed in value and subject to inflation, so what appears to be an adequate sum at one time may purchase considerably less after inflation has set in. A family with an income of $2,000 a year was very comfortable at the turn of the century. Today the average family could barely survive on that income.

Since it is only the purchasing power of money, not money itself, that is important, it is impossible to forecast accurately the *real* value of investments with a fixed return. It is advisable, if possible, in planning for retirement, to provide yourself with a hedge against inflation. One such investment is real estate. If you own your home you already have a measure of protection against inflation, since rent usually increases along with other costs, whereas the size of a mortgage will remain the same. In a period of deflation, however, owning a home might prove unprofitable. Rents would go down, as would salaries, but mortgage payments would not.

Another risk involved in ownership is that by the time you decide to sell your house the neighborhood might have changed and you will have to take less than you originally paid. For some people the time and attention needed to keep a house in good condition becomes too much as they grow older. In general, however, owning a home is protection against inflation.

Before making investments of any kind, especially during retirement, you should have a certain amount of money put aside so that you can get it on short notice in case of an emergency. This can be in the form of a savings account, checking account, or government bonds. A sum equal to about six months' income is advisable. Beyond this amount, money should be invested so as to guarantee as great a return as possible.

In the field of securities there are three general types: bonds, preferred stock, and common stock. There are also mutual funds of different kinds. The New York Stock Exchange publishes a magazine which explains the nature of most of these securities; the library has books available that give detailed information on investing money. The most expedient way, of course, is to consult a professional advisement investor or broker who is recommended (perhaps through a friend or the finance and marketing department of a local college).

What part does Social Security play in your retirement plans? Perhaps you have thought of it only before retirement as a piece out of your salary check, and in retirement as a small monthly addition to your income. Social Security is much more than that. It actually is an insurance policy protecting you against loss of income due to death, disability, and retirement. It's also a health insurance policy when you retire.

Some people assume that Social Security benefits are automatic. They are *not*; they must be applied for. The following information is provided here to help you understand how Social Security works and what it can do for you.*

When you work, your employer deducts a percentage from your salary check and matches it dollar for dollar with his own money. He then sends the combined sum to Social Security Administration headquarters

---

*NOTE: Consult your local Social Security Office for current changes and provisions in Social Security laws and benefits.

where a computer credits the deposit to your account. The money is divided among three funds: the Federal Old-Age and Survivors Insurance Trust Fund, which sends checks to retirees and to the families of workers who are deceased; the Federal Disability Insurance Trust Fund, which sends checks to disabled workers; the Federal Hospital Insurance Trust Fund and the Federal Medical Insurance Fund which pay partial hospital costs of retired people over sixty-five (Medicare).

Although Social Security covers most United States employees, there are a few exceptions. Most federal employees are not covered because they have their own civil service retirement system. Local and state government workers in various districts around the country have voted to operate their own retirement system instead of going under Social Security. Workers for some nonprofit organizations are not covered.

A special benefit goes to retirees who have reached seventy-two before 1968. They can receive Social Security benefits even if they have accumulated no quarters of coverage. How much you contribute depends on your income. The 1975 rates call for a deduction of 5.85 percent of your salary, with your employer putting up a matching sum. (Self-employed people pay 8 percent of their income into the system, sending it to the I.R.S. along with their income tax.) The more you make, the more you pay, and the more credit you build up. How much of your contribution will you get back? A man of sixty-five who retires after forty years of work and contributing the maximum amount (only about $5,000) will receive a monthly Social Security check for $400, or $4,800 a year. If he lives to the age of seventy, he'll have collected $24,000, almost *five* times what he contributed.

What if you have reached retirement age and still want to work? Is it possible to hold a job and still collect Social Security benefits? Yes—up to a point. You can earn up to $2,400 a year without losing any benefits. If you earn over that sum, your checks will be reduced $1 for every $2 you earn. However, beyond the age of seventy-two, you can earn any amount and still receive full benefits. Whatever you get out of Social Security, the important point is that it's *yours*. You paid for the protection and it should be returned when you request it.

Although some people do live on Social Security benefits, in an inflation period it is usually necessary to augment them with other income, such as a savings or pension plan.

The phenomenon of the generous retiree turned "skinflint" is not as rare as might be imagined. Sometimes there is genuine cause, as when there has been little or no preparation for a new and different standard of living. However, if a couple planning retirement some years before map out a working arrangement for their later years, they usually are able to answer the question, "Will I have enough?" with far more confidence than those who just let it happen. If, after advance preparation, they find the answer turns out to be negative, it then may be necessary for them to augment the income with part-time work of a compatible nature. Several of my neighbors have taken on part-time positions, working a few days a week or a few hours a day. They have found that it not only improves their income but gives them a new zest and purpose as "semi-retired" people.

The heading of this chapter refers to more than the economic challenges of retirement living. The question has another ramification: "Will I have enough, not only to live on but to *do?*" For example, how does one manage to include trips and travel on a retirement budget?

If you took an expensive two-week vacation annually when you worked (expensive because you didn't have the time or inclination to hunt for bargains, and two weeks because that's all you got) you may now find that you have more time and inclination, albeit less money.

You may discover many kinds of budget trips by reading travel books and going to travel agencies. There is one super-travel experience I would like to share which has been enjoyed by nonretirees as well as retirees for many years. Formerly this kind of vacation was known only to educators, but you need not be one to benefit by its many inexpensive cultural and recreational activities.

During the months of July and August numerous colleges and universities throw open their doors and campus facilities to those in the community who appreciate what they have to offer. Some of them provide dormitory buildings for the use of both married couples and single people. Universities which do not have such accommodations have a Student Housing Office which will help you track down rooms or apartments close to the campus. Frequently the schools that have available sleeping accommodations require you to take at least a one-credit course (or if you are a couple, that one of you enroll for such a course). This may be audited, which means you may "sit in" on the class without receiving academic credit. Many schools offer reduced tuition rates for students over sixty-five.

I received more than thirty credits at the University

of Rhode Island in Kingston, where we lived in a comfortable garden apartment on campus for three summers and in a dorm for four summers. This was an exciting experience, because I not only benefited from the courses but we became involved in the life of the lovely New England campus. (Incidentally, it was here that I also took my first course in the problems of the aging.)

While you live on or near campus, you will be able to enjoy the concerts, theatre, art and foreign films, museums, libraries, exhibits, lectures, guided tours, and other programs open to the public for a nominal fee or no charge. If you have any free time, you will want to go on short or extended trips to places of interest in the surrounding areas. For example, when we lived in a dorm at the University of Maine in Orono, we spent several delightful weekends exploring parts of Canada which was only two hundred miles away. The following summer, for a change of pace, we traveled across country to the University of Colorado in Boulder, where a whole new adventure in climate, geography, culture, and people awaited us. Another summer, at the University of Wisconsin in Madison, we ate delightful food in the cafeteria and joined students and faculty in classrooms, lecture halls, boat rides, picnics, and dances.

I could write a book just on the wonderful summers we spent in this way, making new friends, learning new things, having new adventures.

Right now we are enjoying our sixth "vacation" at Cornell University in Ithaca, New York, where I am writing this book in one of the most congenial atmospheres imaginable. We have also made friendships in the community which have enriched our adventures in retirement. There is something in the "air" of a college or university town which adds zip and sparkle to those who appreciate its offerings.

Foreign universities provide the same kinds of programs. With careful planning and budgeting one can take a "no-frills" or special charter plane trip to England, Italy, Spain, Mexico, or Canada and then reside at one of the universities for four to eight weeks. At this moment we are planning another such vacation at the University of Edinburgh.

If this relatively inexpensive and rewarding kind of experience turns you on, send a letter of inquiry to the Director of Summer Sessions, in care of the college or university you think you might like to explore. The American Automobile Association, the public library, or your travel agent should be able to give you further information on locations, climate, and topography of the schools and areas of your choice.

CHAPTER VIII

THE SINGLE SCENE

Most books on retirement and/or getting older seem to be addressed most often to couples. This is reasonable, since a majority of married couples do retire together. Yet many persons spend their later years alone. This may have come about through death, divorce, or separation, but it is not the same single state of the twenties or thirties prior to marriage. Another single person who is often overlooked is the one who has never married—the spinster or bachelor who chooses to retire from the working world. What are the problems of men and women who are part of the single scene, and how do they handle them?

A typical situation of the person alone is described by this widow in the first stage of recovery:

> *Dear Ruth:*
> *I became a widow seven months ago after forty years of marriage and find that I have not only lost my*

husband but most of my friends as well.

When my husband was alive, we entertained
frequently and were constantly being invited to our
friends' homes. For the first month or so after my
husband passed away, I received many calls and visits
from sympathetic neighbors. Gradually phone calls and
visits became less and less frequent.

I am still the same person, and I still own the same
nice home in the same neighborhood. Is there any good
reason why I should not be included in at least a few
of the many invitations I received when I had the status
of a wife? Isn't a widow entitled to sympathy and understanding from friends for more than a period of thirty
to sixty days?   Miserable Minna

Dear Minna:

It certainly is easy to comprehend why you are
miserable. Unfortunately your situation is not an unusual
one.

Somehow, no matter how popular two people were as
a couple, the fact remains that half of the couple seems
difficult for some friends to deal with. Our society
generally moves in a pattern of couples which is
particularly cruel to those who were formerly an
accepted part of the pattern.

You are now a "single" once again and will need to
carve out a life-style of your own. You mention a "nice
home" so I assume that you have no pressing financial
problems.

Even so, if you are physically able, try to find yourself
a job of some kind, either full or part time. Be
sure it's one in which you are involved with people
and their problems. In so doing you will see your own
problem fade into the background as time passes.
You will also be able to establish new friendships
and perhaps begin entertaining again, on a small scale.

If you are not interested in employment, volunteer
your time to worthwhile organizations which will
welcome your experience and maturity.

Seek out other singles with whom you share common

interests, so that you need not depend on couples
for dinner and theatre invitations.

Above all, don't stay home and wait for calls from
former friends. When they discover that you are not
moping or miserable they will be more apt to invite
you to their parties. By that time, you will have no need
of your fair-weather friends because you will be leading
a meaningful life of your own.

"Miserable Minna," in the throes of grief and bewilderment, has a way to go in the realistic understanding of her "single" position. Learning to cope with this
new life-style is rough. Reactions range the gamut of
strong emotions, including sorrow, anger, resentment,
fear, irritation, and self-pity. Although the greatest
problem is acceptance of the new status on the part of
the widow or widower, the attitudes of friends and
neighbors may also pose a problem. The following
letter-writer finds herself caught on the horns of an
almost humorous dilemma.

Dear Ruth:

I have been a widow for the past few years, trying
hard to adjust to living alone. It hasn't been easy,
but I managed to keep busy somehow and even made a
few friends, all of them women like myself. I had
about given up ideas of remarrying or having a close
relationship with another man.

Recently I was introduced to an eligible widower
who seemed to take an immediate interest in me. I
certainly was thrilled and flattered because it was a good
feeling to think that a man once more might find me
desirable. When this gentleman called to ask me for a

date, I did not hesitate to accept. As a matter of fact,
I had my hair done in a new style and treated myself
to a new dress for the occasion. I looked forward to
an enjoyable evening with a male companion—an
experience I had missed for a long time.

However, the one thing I never anticipated was the
interest suddenly exhibited by my neighbors and friends.

Ten minutes before my gentleman caller came to the
door, three of my friends decided to drop in to inquire
about my health! After I got rid of them, and my date
and I started for his car, two of my neighbors appeared
in the parking lot waiting to be introduced. The next day,
two or three other friends phoned to inquire how I had
spent the evening.

I hope this new relationship will develop into something worthwhile, but how can I keep it from turning
into an item for gossip and speculation without losing
some of my friends at the same time?

Paula C.

Dear Paula:

In retirement some people are unable to cope with unplanned leisure hours for which there has been little
or no preparation. Consequently the interest they
display in their neighbors' private lives frequently takes
the place, vicariously, of stimulation and challenge in
their own monotonous routines.

You are to be commended for the new romantic
interest in your life after your lonesome period. However,
you are entitled to privacy and dignity, no matter what
kind of relationship this association should develop into.
As a mature and knowledgeable adult, you should be
able to let your neighbors understand this is your own
business—without losing their friendship. It occurs to me,
however, that you must have somehow informed a few
people beforehand that you were anticipating a date
with a member of the opposite sex. Perhaps, subconsciously, you are not really trying to avoid sharing
your pleasure with friends, because that may be part
of this new exciting experience. If you really prefer

to keep your gentleman caller where he can't be seen,
why not try meeting him somewhere else? Then when
the time for making wedding announcements draws
close, you will have the satisfaction of really surprising
all those devoted neighbors and friends!

━━━━━━━━

What are the major problems of most older women in retirement without mates?

The preceding letters, though different, have a common thread running through them—resentment that a widow must create her own social and emotional climate without help. When she is baffled, she cannot turn automatically to her spouse as she has been accustomed. Unless she is living with a close friend, she cannot expect to discuss personal matters as soon as they come up. The widow may frequently find herself in shock, for which she is totally unprepared. Mary Porter had been such a close part of her husband's life that she refused to accept the fact of his death for several weeks. Her friends became concerned when she talked about Harry as if he had gone on an errand and would return at any time. One day she set the table for two, prepared a special dinner, and sat waiting for Harry's key in the door. When the concerned daughter called several hours later, she was horrified to hear her mother crying as if her heart would break. At that moment, the work of mourning had actually begun. The veneer of stoic calm that Mary had preserved for weeks had cracked and the healing process was under way. The next morning when

Mrs. Porter's daughter called, her mother inquired about her grandchild for the first time since the death of her spouse. Mary gradually was able to withdraw the love investment from the deceased and reinvest it in other people. The length of time it takes to do this differs with people. Continued mourning is unhealthy and may reflect guilt, self-pity, or mistaken notions of enduring devotion to a memory. A complex of this kind may result in chronic depression and will usually require professional treatment. An emotionally stable person is able to recover from acute grief caused by the loss of a loved one in a period of time that varies with the individual. A widow who has had a healthy relationship with her spouse is able to resume meaningful relationships with others, even though she may place her first husband in a special recess of her heart.

After all, a husband may have served in many roles in his lifetime—confidant, counselor, guide, companion, "big brother," financial expert, security blanket, and sex partner. Small wonder that he is sorely missed. Before his death there were two people to shoulder responsibilities more or less equally. With the same or more problems, the surviving spouse has only half the amount of brainpower, energy, skill, and cooperation.

Another major problem for most widows is usually that of a reduced income. Although there may be fewer expenses, she may still have to modify her former life-style. Many widows whose husbands managed the family finances all on their own are helplessly panicked by their lack of knowledge. Well-meaning men do a great injustice to their women by choosing to keep them in the dark about financial matters. The kindest and most loving thing an older man can do for his wife is to keep her fully informed as to the provisions he has made for her in case of his death.

The second greatest shock a grieving widow can possibly be hit with is the fact that her husband carried no insurance or hadn't made any other arrangements because he had never been sick in his life and intended to live to a ripe old age. In her moving book, *Widow*, Lynn Caine expressed her misery and disbelief in no uncertain terms when she discovered that her loving husband had left his affairs in a terrible financial mess. Since he had never been ill, the thought of cancer never occurred to him. Like many younger men with a comfortable income, he felt that the future was something to be taken care of in the future. But the future never came for *him*.

His widow and orphaned children had to face it alone. Mrs. Caine suggests the need for a "Contingency Day"—a session between husband and wife wherein the total picture of financial assets and liabilities on the death of a spouse is freely and fully evaluated. She goes further, recommending the consulting of a lawyer and even an acountant. If you think this is morbid, she says, then you are not permitting your mate the opportunity to really show how much he loves you. If he needs encouragement, and most husbands do, don't be afraid that he will misinterpret your practical interest in the future. It is far better to face the inevitable aspects of the future together than to face the horror of an unplanned present alone.

Mrs. Caine was a relatively young woman, and survived her traumatic situation because she was able to continue in her job with a publishing company. Although it was necessary to adhere to a strictly curtailed budget, she found mental solace and adequate financial independence for her family and herself. What does an *older* woman do when she suddenly becomes a widow and discovers, after all medical and funeral costs have been defrayed, that there is not much left on which to live? Unless she is in ill health, it will be necessary for her to call on all her inner resources and decide how she can best add to her limited income. If she has never worked, it will be difficult but not impossible for her to find a job suited to her limited skills. One of my students, after sizing up the situation, approached a friend for a loan to finance a course in shorthand and typing. Several months later she was able to start repaying the loan because she had landed a job in a local insurance office where her mature appearance and pleasant personality were a distinct asset to her employer.

By far the most difficult adjustment for separated, divorced, and widowed persons to make is learning to live alone again. Even after an incompatible relationship has been dissolved, there is a sense of loss and insecurity that lasts for varying periods of time, according to the individual. Very few widowed persons who have had a poor relationship ever acknowledge that they are inwardly experiencing a sense of relief at their mate's passing, whereas divorced people can openly express their feelings, no matter how strong they are.

For most people, living alone seems unnatural unless they have always done so. Adult children frequently mean well, but they are unable to fill the gap. Usually they have lives of their own, in which the best loved parent feels he has no essential part or purpose. Occasionally in the first shock that follows dissolution of a parental home, a son or daughter offers the survivor a home. Although I have known of one or two fairly successful arrangements like this, it is far better not to succumb to what appears to be the answer to loneliness in the first flush of bereavement.

I recall my sense of dismay and rejection when my just-widowed mother-in-law refused to sell her home and come to live with us. We had always had such a warm relationship that I could not understand why she would not want to share our family life. It was not until some years had passed and I watched her retain her independence and dignity in her own familiar surroundings that I finally realized how very wise she was.

In our retirement area, I have observed that widows, far more than widowers, begin to enjoy their single state as soon as the sharp edges of grief have worn off. This is true, even though widows are slower to socialize and date than widowers. In our discussion groups, some widows and divorced women agreed that they enjoyed their freedom, once they had adjusted to it, and preferred not to remarry. Widowers, divorced men, and a few bachelors were more interested in finding an agreeable arrangement with a compatible female (not always marriage). The need for domestic comfort and companionship seems to be felt more strongly by men than women. In some cases, a bachelor or widower would move in with a spinster or widowed sister and maintain an atypical but mutually helpful household. This also seems to work well financially, since sharing food, rent, furniture, entertainment, and other costs can result in a higher standard of living for both.

Although there is a tendency to confuse being alone with loneliness, they are not the same thing. The fear of loneliness sometimes catapults people into situations they really don't want. Loneliness creates feelings of despair and misery, of being cut off from warmth and companionship. Being alone—as was indicated by well-adjusted singles—simply means living comfortably by oneself, by choice. Some single people panic when they are alone, believing that they must also be lonely. The truth of the matter is that there are singles who have learned to live alone and find there is no need to be lonesome, which is a different matter.

One of my neighbors, an ex-teacher who was widowed several years ago, leads a social life that some married women might envy. She is rarely at home, except when she entertains friends. And she has friends whom she has made on the golf course, at the community center, and in the various clubs and organizations she has joined. She is welcomed by other widows and married couples alike because she is a charming social asset with a friendly, helpful attitude toward both sexes that commands affection and respect. Although she is not rejecting the idea of marriage and goes out on dates, she seems to be quite content with the life she leads. In her spare time, she reads avidly, paints in oils, and goes bowling. She lives alone—but she is not lonely. The last time I talked with her, she was planning an extensive trip to the Orient by freighter. Ellen has lived through loneliness and now lives alone through choice.

Chuck, a bachelor in his fifties, has been very much in demand by hostesses because he makes a highly desirable "extra man." It has always been flattering to be invited to dinners and cocktail parties and be sought after by ladies, both married and unmarried. Lately, despite his great social life, Chuck started to feel strangely depressed and lonely. One Saturday night he came home late after a hectic round of partying, looked around his tastefully furnished "pad," and almost burst into tears. He suddenly realized there wasn't a single person he really cared about or who cared deeply for him. All his friends were party friends with superficial interests. He couldn't recall one meaningful conversation he had ever had with any one of them. At that point he decided he was ready for another way of life. The following week he registered for an extension course in creative writing at a neighborhood college. He had always wanted to write but had never taken the time to do it. Six months later he had made some new friends with whom he shared similar interests and was writing some pretty good fiction. He stayed home several evenings a week writing. He was alone, but for the first time in his life he was enjoying it. Sure, he still goes to parties, but he has something to talk about with his new friends when they get together.

The older widower or divorced man usually has choices about his new life-style. Normally he does not find as many things to do around a home as does a widow or divorcee. In most cases he is not a very competent housekeeper, cook, or laundryman. Frequently he is pressured into an early remarriage because of his need for a homemaker more than anything else. This may possibly account for some of the reluctance on the part of widows to remarry.

Mollie, a buxom widow of independent means, expressed it bluntly in class one day: "I'll be darned if I'll start cooking big meals and mending socks for some spoiled old codger who's just getting married for his own convenience!"

Divorced men, after a thorough fling at freedom,

usually tend to seek another marital partner. Although age has a lot to do with it, there are widowers who openly resent being viewed as potential "bait" for eligible single women.

A dignified, gray-haired gentleman just turned seventy, George is an example of a widower who prefers to live with his memories. "Agnes and I had a happy marriage for almost fifty years. I haven't the slightest intention of trying to replace her for any reason. I don't dislike the ladies, but one wife in a lifetime is enough for me." George lives comfortably in an apartment hotel with maid service and meals. He spends most of his evenings playing chess and reading in the lounge.

Although George and a few of his contemporaries choose an uneventful course, most singles overcome this stage after a normal period of withdrawal. Conventionally, it has always been easier for a man to ask a woman for a date, although if he has been out of circulation for years, the first time may be awkward. Many a widow or divorcee, though she is supposed to be flattered when asked, is also uncomfortable for the same reason. Depending on how long it has been, both wonder how to act, what to say, how far to go, etc. "Coming on strong" has wrecked a number of relationships on a first evening out.

Alice is an attractive widow in her late fifties who told me that she has started avoiding dates with a man alone unless she knows him very well.

"Even though they are old enough to know better, they make sexual advances on the first or second date as if they were teen-agers. Why does a man act as if he's God's gift to a woman when she doesn't really know him?"

Perhaps some men feel that making overtures to a lady is expected and that they appear more virile when they at least try. Some Romeos, if the truth be told, may not be too upset inwardly when a date politely declines romance on brief acquaintance. The need for affection and companionship does not lessen with advancing years for either sex. Whether they will admit it or not, there are a number of older women and men who would be just as content to enjoy a mutually compatible association without sex. On the other hand, some later marriages are a blissful combination of sexual, mental, and temperamental compatibility enriched by the mellow experiences each partner has brought to the union.

The chances of success in a second marriage vary with the people involved, as well as other factors such as the reasons for the second marriage. Sometimes singles marry because they are lonely and expect marriage to result in miracles. It doesn't. Those who have profited from experience work harder at their second union than their first. If there are no serious problems and a sincere desire exists to make it work, the new marriage can be rewarding. The newly widowed or divorced person has to be especially cautious about not rushing into anything because he is unhappy and alone. A good reason for waiting to do anything different or unusual is obvious. A divorced single is often hurt and humiliated. A widowed single is shocked and grieved. In either case, it is important to use a cooling-off (or warming-up) period to return to an acceptance of one's self as a whole person. When the healing process is complete and the single person has returned to society, he or she is then ready for all kinds of new experiences, whatever they may be.

A discussion of the single scene would not be complete

without consideration of those singles who want to find other singles. To many, society seems to be made up of married couples, but they may want only to make new friendships and have a more fulfilling life.

There are singles who are not strictly sex and/or mate oriented, but they are worried that others will *think* they are if they join singles clubs. They feel some sort of stigma is attached to the idea. When a group of single persons in our complex formed such a club, two or three women turned down an invitation to join. Mabel, a small, peppy widow in her fifties, said, "I have enough interests to keep me busy without joining a club that has only one purpose."

Mabel is an unusually independent, self-sufficient person with many inner resources. She may be wrong about one thing, however. Moving in, and with, a group of singles is a practical and comforting thing to do for some who are adjusting to a new status. Not all singles groups function in the same way, but all of them provide companionship and motivation to most of their members. The attitude with which a single looks at his or her situation is of primary importance.

If you are a single you have to decide that you are going to create a new way of life, new friends, and new experiences, and one of the best ways to do this is to become involved. Political and community clubs, church and ethnic groups, charitable and social organizations are good places to get started.

Another area to explore is the encounter group. Large numbers of singles are attracted to these workshop and discussion sessions. You may have to search until you find the right one for you; if you do, you will probably benefit by the give-and-take of encounter and sharing of experiences with other people.

Another stimulating way to get involved is to try to learn a new skill by joining a hobby club or taking a course in adult education. Incidentally you will meet new people this way, but you will also benefit by venturing into a new field. There are few things as exciting as becoming part of a community drive or a political campaign. You may find you have a talent or ability that's been hidden all these years. Besides, working with people who have similar interests and ideas gives anyone a satisfying feeling of purpose and identity.

If your town or community has no organized singles group, you might try calling a dozen congenial people and forming your own. You will be surprised at the warm reception it will receive from most lonely singles. When you get together, you can decide if your group will have any function other than social. You may even be able to draw a Mabel into the singles group by having her "volunteer" as program chairman.

If you have read this chapter and are a new single, you may possibly react to some of these suggestions with disbelief, skepticism, or bitterness. In your personal crisis, you may not believe anything will work. I don't blame you...but you *must* believe that this is only a stage. You *must* believe that you will gradually emerge from it and take up a new life-style. If you keep working at it, one day after the other, you will ultimately find the way, and the very first step is to stop thinking so much about *yourself* and your own plight. Somehow you become a more interesting and enlightened person when you become interested in others. Your face, your body, your personality will become more animated and therefore more attractive. Others before you have found the way back. So can you.

CHAPTER IX

THE LIBERATED SEX

Men—and some women—believe that men are the truly liberated sex. It seems to me that with all the furor over women's liberation one major item has been overlooked. If men have always been liberated, why do statistics indicate that they have more heart attacks, more nervous breakdowns, more criminal records, more suicides, and earlier deaths?

Young men are too busy to pay much attention to these facts. They may be vaguely disturbed but are too caught up in making money to do any serious thinking about it. Only when they get older do they begin to suspect that maybe they are not as liberated as they like to believe.

Few men talk about their personal feelings, but when they do, startling attitudes are revealed. Older men are more depressed about themselves, in general, than are older women. Having been brought up in a generation that stressed the image of the strong, self-sufficient, virile man, they become inwardly frustrated if they are unable to live up to that stereotype.

A boy growing up in the first half of the twentieth century was expected to be a "real man." There were certain things a "real man" was to do: protect women, no matter how afraid he was inside; be strong (never cry or show deep emotion); have powerful biceps (and if he didn't, he was expected to work at developing them). He knew that one of his most important goals in life was to make as much money as possible, because one day he would marry and have to support a family. Potential sexual ability was a constant topic of conversation among his youthful peers. His parents, his teachers, his friends, his sweetheart, and eventually his wife continually told him he was "the greatest" if he lived up to all these expectations.

So what of the man who didn't have a lot of muscle, a lot of money, or a strong sex drive? What if he occasionally was moved to cry? Frequently he buried these feelings as he grew up and tried harder to press himself into the mold created by society. Most men succeeded—at least outwardly conforming to what was expected.

Most men go along doing what they are expected to do. And then one day, something happens that starts them thinking. The men in our discussion groups were encouraged to talk about it.

Dave, a thin, sensitive man past sixty, smiled as he recounted an incident. "I was late for work and ran for the bus that took me to the subway station. As usual it was crowded, but I found a place to stand in front of an attractive young woman. I must have been breathing hard, but I almost fainted when she got up and offered me her seat."

When the laughter subsided, Milton, a well-groomed man in his late fifties, said he had been shopping in the men's wear department of a local store and asked a young saleslady for assistance in selecting a sport jacket. "I have just the thing for you, sir," she said, and brought forth a sedate, dark-blue jacket she obviously thought appropriate for a man his age. "I was depressed all day after that happened. Imagine anyone thinking I'd be caught *dead* in a jacket like that!"

It is much easier for women to express themselves, because they are expected to do so. Part of the male image used to include the silent stoic but, fortunately, this picture is changing. When I asked several men questions about themselves and told them their answers would be included in this chapter, they were quite co-operative.

A number of them told me that they no longer feel needed or useful as they are getting older. "My wife always has something to do," one man said. "Even though the children are no longer home she's always busy with one thing or another. I just sit around and feel I'm getting in the way. If I thought I could get another job I would go back to work."

It is apparent that many men's feelings of worth are strongly attached to their appearance, their physical condition, and earning power. Sometimes a man who has looked forward to later life as a time of financial security and respected status becomes suddenly aware that his years of carefully acquired knowledge and experience are no longer held in high regard.

Harvey, a portly middle-aged man, confessed that he started to feel insecure when a thirty-year-old "youngster" became vice-president of his firm. "It was the first time I realized how easily I could be replaced. This kid had a master's degree in business administration and talked like a college professor. Despite all my experience I felt like an old fuddy-duddy next to him."

Men have other feelings that tend to prove they are not the liberated sex they're supposed to be. The following was told to my husband by a former college friend he met at an alumni reunion. "Janey and I were high school sweethearts when we got married. We had four kids in six years, and I've been working steadily to pay for shoes, braces, and books. I've never had time to know another woman, and I'm beginning to think I've missed the boat."

This is more than a symptom of the "seven-year itch" supposedly felt by married men. This is the story of the average American male who feels life closing in on him and doesn't know how it happened. At the other end is the man who occasionally takes a fling at adultery but even then is not rewarded by a sense of real liberation. He is forcing himself to accept false values that usually result in guilt and frustration.

For some older men who experience severe inner problems, copping out appears to be the only answer. I recall how our neighborhood was rocked years ago by the scandal of a respectable physician who ran off to the South Pacific with his nurse, deserting his wife and family after more than thirty years. What added an unusual touch to this particular episode was that the nurse was fifty-two years old, about the same age as the doctor's wife. In the gossip that followed, I also remember the remark made by one of the neighbors. "I could see him going off with a *young* girl, but why did he leave her for such a plain woman as Miss Jones...and her old enough to know better!"

How little most of us know about the men and women we see all the time! Frequently a man does not have another male friend in whom he can freely confide. He may not want to burden his wife with his fears and disappointments because he thinks it will alter his image in her eyes. Since American men of an earlier generation were taught to keep feelings to themselves, it has been difficult for them to unburden themselves to other men for fear they will be labeled effeminate. It is a rare American male who can have a close relationship with another male without worrying that he will be thought of as homosexual. The only places I have seen men embracing warmly and engaging in lengthy conversations were in Rome, Paris, and Athens. I wouldn't be surprised to learn that our former doctor chose an older traveling companion rather than a young one because he needed someone with whom he could be comfortable.

Some men who have liberated wives may experience a sense of frustration because it damages their own concept of a "real man." A good deal of harm may result in a relationship where an older man is not prepared for the advent of women's liberation in his marriage. Frank started having violent headaches when Lillian was elected president of a national organization that required her attention several after-noons and evenings a week. Reared with the archaic notion that women were the inferior sex, Frank was not able to accept the idea that "the little woman" was not only competent but even superior in a position formerly occupied by a man. The truly liberated man is also able to liberate those closest him with no fear of damaging his male image or ego.

Occasionally there is the problem of the man whose wife makes him into a puppet and manipulates him for "his own good." One of the most unpleasant things to witness is the sheepish acquiescence of the husband who tries to please his spouse in all things. The matriarchal woman in the guise of a "good wife" tells her husband what's good for him. She picks out his clothes, she selects his barber, she orders his food from the restaurant menu, she tells him how to drive, she tells him how much to tip (or how little if the waitress is pretty), she pats him on the back when he says something witty, and she probably tucks him in at night. I know of a brilliant college professor whose backbone has been completely removed in this way by his loving helpmate. Recently he was asked to give a lecture on—you guessed it—women's liberation!

If we tried to analyze the professor's situation, we would probably discover a dominating mother in the background. Never having been liberated as a young man, he is apparently content in marriage with this continuation of feminine authority. I would not be too surprised, however, if one of these days he decides to join Dr. Brown in the South Pacific.

Centuries ago, liberated men circumnavigated the globe in search of new worlds to conquer. There are still a few explorers, but the territory has changed to outer space. For the average American male, however, liberation needs to take other forms. He can no longer afford to put all his "egos in one basket," especially as he grows older.

Instead of striving harder to be more masculine the sane and sensitive man needs to care more about being a whole person. We can understand (although not agree with) the urge of a nineteen-year-old to be an "athlete" in most areas of his life, whether on the tennis court or in the bedroom. It is neither wise nor satisfying for the older male to keep pursuing this image. The liberated older man should broaden and refine his image, not discard it. There is no need for a man past sixty to surrender his dynamism and masculine charm. And he won't if he directs his experience and ability into meaningful channels rather than into pale imitations of the male stereotype.

There has been some movement recently around the country which indicates a marked reaction among older men toward their own liberation. Small groups are getting together in adult education and community-oriented sessions to air their feelings about masculine identity. One such course was given last year in a New York suburb; it was called "Mr.: To Be a Man." The ages of the men who enrolled in the course ranged from forty-three to sixty-six.

A recurrent theme was the desire to talk with other men, to become aware of them as individuals, and to clarify their own problems as males in a changing society. Some noteworthy changes occurred in the lives of several of these men as a result. An accountant sold part of his practice to gain more time for himself; an editor entered into therapy; a divorced businessman dissolved an unsatisfactory love affair; an engineer told his wife how he really felt about the unemployed brother who had been living with them.

The real changes, though, were internal. One fifty-year-old manufacturer explained, "This is the first time I ever 'rapped' with other men about intimate problems." A fifty-three-year-old salesman was even more direct: "I learned that I can be honest about my innermost feelings. If I'm hurt or upset, it's okay to cry if I want to." And a sixty-one-year-old pharmacist said, "I am finally beginning to react according to my feelings as a *person*, not as a man."

In coming decades intelligent older men will continue to direct feelings, ideas, and actions toward this new concept of their own liberation.

Right now, however, books and speakers on women's liberation rarely deal with women past the age of fifty...and men are virtually ignored. The art of liberation, like so many other areas, does not seem to warrant consideration in the later stages of life.

―――――

How do older women feel about women's liberation? Many of my generation feel that they are completely out of it—that it applies only to their daughters. They appear content to continue in the same feminine role they have filled for decades. It is much more comfortable not to make waves at this stage, and many husbands agree with them. Yet there are enough women who are not too old to be curious, to ask questions, to be concerned, and even to become involved.

Betty, an outgoing woman in her mid-fifties, felt that older women are definitely being affected by the liberation movement and that their husbands cannot be left out of it. "Bill and I argue a lot over liberation, but we take opposite viewpoints. He feels women still belong in the home, and I want to be more than just a wife, a mother, and a grandmother." Betty admitted that this is a recent development in her life. A few other women admitted that they envy their daughters and daughters-in-law who are successful careerists.

Shirley, a motherly looking woman, had a puzzled expression on her face. "I don't understand my son's willingness to do laundry, dishes, and baby-sitting while my daughter-in-law does her own thing. He may be liberating his wife, but what's going to happen to *him?*"

A man and wife in our discussion group told of their experience.

"Sylvia and I are learning to liberate each other as we grow older. She has found many interests outside the home the last few years and so have I," commented Sid, a retired lawyer. "She is just as feminine, and I feel just as masculine. We feel it's making better *people* out of both of us."

It seems to me that Sylvia and Sid accurately sum up the solution to the problem of liberation of both sexes at any age. We must leave room for growth and expansion for women and men, especially as they grow older. It is pointless for women to cast men as the adversary and vice versa. There is no reason to ignore one sex in favor of the other.

In attempting to weigh the pros and cons of the sexual revolution, I find it has posed more problems for men than for women. Women have moved out and added to their roles; they seem able to do this capably at almost any age, for they haven't had to give up their traditional places. Men have had to adapt to totally new concepts and watch the myths about their own masculinity being destroyed. The older man, in particular, may become more confused about his role, because his job, his status as father and lover, his physical capacities are all being threatened. An older woman, though her children have left home, is still important and necessary in any role she chooses to adopt. Even if she becomes a divorcee or a widow, she generally maintains a home and a status that for an older man would present problems.

One sex cannot be truly liberated until the other is. Shirley's son is liberated enough to free his wife and, despite his mother's concern, this young couple will derive mutual benefit from the arrangement. It is unfortunate that Shirley is so set in her own fixed life-style that she is threatened by the concept of total liberation.

What the world needs now is not women's liberation or men's liberation but *human* liberation.

CHAPTER X

THE OLD FOLKS AT HOME

In the latter part of the twentieth century it is not uncommon to find that the "old folks" are no longer at home. In previous generations, parents remained in the house where they had reared their families, and married children usually settled close by. Those who did not marry frequently stayed on in the same household, taking care of the parents as they grew older. Since most people did not survive into their eighties or nineties, their children never needed to worry about them.

In the last few decades a new complication has arisen. Never before has there been a generation of sexagenarians who are facing, along with their aging parents, the crisis of survival in a society that is unprepared for this phenomenon. Hundreds of thousands of American families are now caught up in a five-level syndrome created by earlier marriages among young

145

people and longer lives for older people.

A typical example is the Ellison family. Jack and Sheila, in their late forties, have three children. Jack's parents, in their sixties, have just retired. Jack's grandmother is a spry eighty-three-year-old living in Miami. Jack's oldest daughter was married two years ago and has just given birth to a baby girl. Mr. and Mrs. Ellison, Sr., are the fourth level in this five-generation family. This picture is becoming increasingly more typical as we head into the twenty-first century.

Right now, however, it is the generation in the sixties that is facing the most unique problem of all. Forty-year-olds are accustomed to having parents in their sixties, but most sixty-year-old couples have never before had to deal with the social, emotional, and economic problems of their parents.

In our retirement community we constantly hear concerned sons and daughters in their fifties, sixties, and even seventies discuss the conflicts they are experiencing with aged parents. The "children" are troubled about their parents' state of health, their living arrangements, their financial straits, their eccentricities, their dependence *or* independence, even their marital problems. Most of the retirees want their parents to be as happy, secure, and comfortable as possible, but many of them don't want to have their own lives disrupted.

When they retired, Marion and Harold bought a two-bedroom, two-bathroom condominium so that Marion's seventy-nine-year-old mother could live with them. Since their finances did not permit separate establishments, this seemed an expedient arrangement. At seventy-nine, Marion's mother was an active woman with a mind of her own. During the first year of this arrangement, she cleaned her own room, did her own cooking, made friends, and enjoyed an independent social life. As time went on, however, Harold was annoyed to find his mother-in-law becoming increasingly dependent. Since she could not drive, he had to take her to the doctor, to the supermarket, and to her twice-weekly card game. At the beginning, she had waited for the local bus until one day she got caught in the rain and came down with a severe cold. Marion was chagrined to discover that her mother was messing up her orderly kitchen and did not always stay in her own room when they were entertaining. Since she loved her mother she also felt guilty when they went off on weekends occasionally, leaving her alone. She tried to arrange for neighbors to check on her mother but was never really at ease until they returned. At present, although the same conditions exist, Harold is no longer the patient, understanding son-in-law; he has become a short-tempered, petulant husband who feels he is "stuck" with an aging mother-in-law.

Another couple we know also arranged to have a parent share their home when her spouse died. In this case, there are a couple of lively teen-agers still living at home. The grandmother is a shy, sensitive woman who tries to solve the problem by getting out of the house as much as possible. Her children know that noise and rock music are making her miserable but feel the kids will resent Grandma if they are made to change their habits. So Grandma moves around like a little gray shadow on the periphery of her children's lives. In past years, grandparents seldom lived long and three generations would "put up" with their personal annoyances and discomfort until obituaries solved the problem. Now that increased longevity is to be expected, however, it becomes more and more important that fifty- and sixty-year-old children and their parents work out more compatible life-styles. The ones that worked for earlier generations are not always successful for the complex "now" generation.

How can a middle-aged husband and wife reconcile their relationships with those of aging parents? They may ask, "Should they live with us, or can they still manage alone? How can we get brothers and sisters to help share the problems? What if they are considering remarriage? Is it right for us to live at a great distance? Where can we get professional help for parents who need it? What about nursing homes?"

Very few middle-aged children are able to sustain a healthy relationship living with an aged parent. This is completely understandable when one considers that for the "children" these may be the years when they had hoped to retire, perhaps to travel. No matter how loving they may be, they invariably come to resent the intrusion of a dependent mother or father. And, just as invariably, the aging parent becomes aware of what is happening and grows crochety, sullen, or miserable. Middle-aged children do not become models of patience and understanding any more than their elderly parents can be expected to become more agreeable and tolerant as they grow older. What I'm saying is that I am *not* in favor of squeezing elderly parents into the same household as their middle-aged children.

If given a choice, most elderly parents don't really want to live under the same roof with middle-aged children. How can thinking older persons enjoy becoming their children's "children"?

Mrs. Dixon, a bright-eyed little octogenarian, lives in

a two-room apartment within walking distance of her daughter and son-in-law. She is pleased about her independence, and her children are proud of her. She has a limited income but manages to keep her place tidy and inviting. The relationship between the two generations is close and affectionate, but Mrs. Dixon has no illusions about the reason.

"My son-in-law Henry enjoys eating my chicken soup as long as I cook it in my own kitchen. I know Alice loves me dearly, but she wants to gad about with Henry and not have to worry about her mother. I may not have a big place, but it's mine and I'm going to keep it until the day I die." Incidentally, Mrs. Dixon enjoys entertaining people her age in the privacy of her own home. She enjoys watching her own television programs without fear of disturbing anyone else. Her daughter and son-in-law delight in bringing their grandchildren to visit Great-grandma, but Mrs. Dixon breathes a sigh of relief when they leave and she can take a nap.

When the surviving parent is male a typical concern is: "How will Dad ever be able to take care of himself?" The following letter is an example of the reaction of a middle-aged daughter to her father's situation.

Dear Ruth:

We are faced with the problem of an aged parent who is the survivor of a long and happy marriage. My father is in his late seventies. When my mother passed away, he was in such a despondent state that we insisted he come and live with us.

Things went well while we both worked, since we were out of the house most of the day. My father took long walks, looked up old friends, read the papers, did some of the shopping, and seemed content.

When we decided to retire, there was no question that

*we would continue the same arrangement. However,
after some months of living together, where we are
constantly in each other's company, we are beginning to
realize that this is not a very healthy situation.*

*We have very little privacy and feel guilty when we
do not include my father in our plans. He does not
complain, but rarely leaves the house to go out unless
we take him. He is in good health, and we cannot
suggest a senior citizens' home or anything like that
because he would be heartbroken.*

*If we continue this way, we feel our own relationship
is bound to suffer. How can we solve this problem
without hurting my father or our marriage?*

Devoted Daughter

Dear Devoted:

*You and your husband are to be commended for the
loving concern you have shown for your father. Although
it was certainly a warm and spontaneous gesture when
you offered a bereaved parent a home, obviously the
result was not what you had anticipated.*

*It is natural for the survivor of the kind of union
you describe to go through a period of grief and
depression. In most cases, this is a stage which is not
too lasting and from which the person emerges to make
his individual adjustments.*

*Although you were moved by compassion in offering
your father a home, you may have unknowingly supplied
him with a "crutch." It is probable that if he were
unable to lean on you he would ultimately have
learned to lean on himself.*

*Research on widows and widowers who do not have
health or economic problems indicates that they manage
to live quite comfortably and independently. You say
that your father kept himself busy while you were both
away. The chances are that he would arrange to be even
more occupied if he were assured of unlimited freedom.
Perhaps he might even like it at this point!*

*With the kind of relationship you appear to have,
why not sit down with your father and talk it over? You*

*may discover that he would not object to a small
apartment in the same neighborhood where you are
welcome to visit or arrange to go out together on
occasion.*

*He may even be ready for a residence hotel where he
can enjoy the company of contemporaries with similar
interests and activities. Perhaps he has not complained
because he does not want to hurt you.*

*Don't underestimate your father. Having recovered
from his initial shock and grief, he may welcome an
arrangement other than the one that was most expedient
in the past.*

*You certainly owe it to yourself and your father
to explore the alternatives. As long as you handle
your problem with honesty and TLC you should be able
to work it out satisfactorily for all concerned.*

Mildred and Paul were not upset when his folks,
ages seventy-eight and eighty-three, refused to move in
with them. Although Paul's mother has failing eyesight,
her husband is able to help her with the housework
and do most of the shopping. Mildred and Paul call
and visit them regularly, often bringing food which
they especially enjoy but which Paul's mother can no
longer prepare. The elderly parents are able to maintain
their independence and still know that their children are
close and understanding. It is easy for middle-aged
children to invade the province of aging parents because
they are worried about their safety. However, as long as
parents *want* to live alone, their children should make
it easier for them by helping as much as they can
for as long as possible.

I have a middle-aged friend who sends her cleaning lady to her mother's house every other week. This thoughtful gift relieves a physical burden and can be accepted with dignity. Marcia's eighty-seven-year-old mother would never permit her daughter to clean her house, but she is not disturbed by the presence of hired help. The sight of spotless floors and clean windows is a never ending source of happiness to the elderly woman.

While I would encourage most middle-aged children to avoid living with elderly parents, some may ask, "What can we do with a parent who is fearful of living alone?"

Norma's seventy-six-year-old mother became hysterical when, shortly after her husband's death, Norma gently urged her to try living alone. "How can you leave your mother alone at a time like this? I never thought I'd see the day when my own child wouldn't want me!"

I sympathized with Norma when she told me of this painful incident, but I certainly admire the way she finally worked it out. She was able to recognize what would happen if she acceded to her mother's wish in a rush of strong emotion. Her mother had always managed a large household and assisted her husband in his retail business. In Norma's home, she would have had to share a bedroom with a nineteen-year-old granddaughter and struggle to put up with telephones, hair dryers, and midnight snacks. Norma invited her mother for a weekend when the nineteen-year-old was having a costume party. Maybe it was a harsh thing to do, but Mrs. Engle was happy to return to the peace and quiet of her own place. After that she rarely came to visit for more than an afternoon in her daughter's busy house. In the last few months,

Mrs. Engle has become a Gray Lady at the local hospital and feels very much needed. Furthermore, she has met an agreeable woman and plans to invite her to move in to share her home.

Up to this point I have been discussing the problems of dealing with elderly parents who have maintained reasonably good health. But what should be done about a parent who is not well and requires more care and attention than can be provided at home? What about a parent who should enter a nursing home or other institution? Those who have been through this ordeal know that it can be a most harrowing and exhausting experience. The son or daughter who must make such a decision often experiences a deep sense of guilt. The fact that he or she may someday be in the same position plays a subconscious part. "How would I feel if *my* child tried to do this to me?"

Unfortunately, the decision to institutionalize an elderly parent is usually made in a time of crisis. Very few middle-aged people themselves make their own provisions for the future when they are of sane mind and active body. I know one gentleman who, much to the amazement of family and friends alike, worked out his personal destiny long before there was a need. Mr. Klein was in his early seventies when he made the rounds of senior citizen residences and nursing homes all over the city. His purpose was to find the best one himself before there was a need for his children to do it. At the age of seventy-seven, after recovering from a hip injury, Mr. Klein signed himself into a home for the aged which he had carefully investigated. Some of his friends were already there and welcomed his arrival with a party. It did not take Mr. Klein long to become something of a leader, working with the social service director in the home, arranging game nights, showing slides of his travels, and starting a discussion group. Mr. Klein is a most unusual senior citizen, but I wonder if more of us could not benefit by his far-sighted example. Why shouldn't an older person have as much right to select an institution as any other type of living arrangement? There are elderly people who do not require medical care but simply want a pleasant atmosphere, sociability, meals, and mild activity. As far as the economic expenditure in Mr. Klein's case, I was later informed by his oldest son (sixty) that he and his two brothers had arranged to share the cost of maintaining their father in the home. Although the first reaction was one of dismay, Mr. Klein's children soon realized that their father could never have adjusted in their homes. It is important for the middle-aged to respect the wish of aging parents to reside with peers rather than with a member of the family.

Another type of semi-institution that meets the needs of some elderly people is the day care center for the old. In the last decade these and senior citizen centers have been flourishing in many cities around the country. New York City has more than a hundred which serve as a kind of halfway house to institutions. Some of them are run by the Department of Social Services; others are privately operated and funded by charitable or religious organizations.

I visited one Senior Citizens' Center on Kings Highway in Brooklyn, New York, where my mother-in-law became an outstanding contributing member after the sudden death of her husband. Having been a teacher in her youth and a vigorous, intelligent woman all her life, she insisted on maintaining her own home on a quiet street in Flatbush. The Kings Highway Center soon became her home away from home. From the age of sixty-eight to eighty-two she spent many happy hours there as editor of the Center bulletin, discussion leader, dinner hostess, and artist. Under the supervision of trained and volunteer personnel, this center has become a well-organized source of hot lunches, companionship, instructional and cultural programs, and other services for older people of both sexes. It was here that Esther Turk, who had never held a brush in her hand, learned to paint in oils and watercolors at the age of sixty-eight. I met many other men and women at the Center during the years my mother-in-law was a member. Most of them were elderly people who seemed to have achieved new meaning in their daily lives. Some of them would have become housebound and decrepit if they had not had the Center to go to every day. Some of the most exciting programs for the elderly I ever saw were the ones in which the Center members sang, recited, danced, and acted for their middle-aged visiting children on holiday occasions. I must point out that many of the participants had ailments of various kinds, but they seemed to overlook them while they were at the Center. These same people would have deteriorated if they had remained at home with only their self-centered thoughts for company.

Another senior center with which I became involved last summer is the one on North Geneva Street in Ithaca, New York. Although this is not a large metropolitan organization, it is an excellent example of what can be accomplished in a small city through the efforts of the community and its active elderly citizens. Located in an attractive two-story white house on a tree-lined street, the Senior Citizen Center for the past three years has become a focal point for the growing elderly population. Prior to this time, Tompkins County residents over the age of sixty-five had few social and activity centered sources other than those provided by religious and private affiliations. Recently the Center has offered elderly people in the area a program of arts and crafts, square dancing, singalongs, language classes, guest speakers, picnics, outings, and organized trips to places of interest. Funded as it is by businessmen in the community, the Center has operated on a limited budget thus far. Nevertheless, a full-time director has just been hired, and plans for an extended program of activities are under way. The men and women I met there on Thursday afternoons when I guided rap sessions on problems of getting older were all alert, bright-eyed, and eager to be involved. I was particularly impressed by two white-haired women who showed up early at every meeting. It was not until the third session that I learned that Edna was totally blind and that her companion had partial vision in one eye. These two women share an apartment in a housing complex for senior citizens down the street; they manage to attend most of the activities at the center, rain or shine. They are beautiful examples of independent spirits who refuse to succumb to physical limitations. As long as there is a place in which to be involved, handicapped or not, many older people will continue to go.

I know that some gerontologists disapprove of segregated community centers for the elderly, asserting that it deprives them of interaction with the young, and therefore is unhealthy. From what I have observed, most people are usually more comfortable with their own peers, whatever their age. However, I agree that there should be freedom of choice in living arrangements, if at all possible. This also applies to choice of friends, activities, cultural pursuits, and other areas of an individual's life-style.

Earlier in this chapter, I mentioned that there might be a need for middle-aged children to consider a nursing home for parents who have become so sick or disabled that they cannot live alone or with anyone else. I now realize that I skirted this important issue because of the unpleasant feelings it arouses. When an elderly parent is acutely ill, the filial emotions are usually so painful that no well-meaning book read in advance can have any effect during the crisis. Those involved will do the best they can under the circumstances, following the doctor's recommendation and making certain that the nursing home is licensed by the state and is adequately staffed. An institution that is nationally accredited under the Joint Commission on Accreditation observes more stringent standards than those set forth by state legislatures; quality care can be expected in such a place.

If it becomes necessary for you to take sick parents to the hospital do everything you possibly can to alleviate their fears and anxiety, but don't treat them like children. Sometimes a childhood fear of hospitals will be reactivated in older persons' memories so that it is necessary to reassure them and let them feel that you have faith in their recovery—but do not overact. It is easy for parents to "see through" their own child. Something for the middle-aged "child" also to remember is that illness at an advanced age is not necessarily fatal. Medical care and treatment, though not always 100 percent effective, can be helpful in returning the patient to a state of relative health for a period of time.

I know of a spry eighty-one-year-old who had a bad fall on the golf course and sustained a severe back injury. While in the hospital, Alex developed pneumonia, and the family began to worry that he would not make it. Though it took months for Alex to recover, his own cheerful attitude and well-preserved body, combined with excellent treatment, helped to put him back on his beloved golf course the following season. In the last four years he has been as chipper and active as he was before the accident.

Occasionally middle-aged children are surprised and concerned when an elderly parent displays an interest in the opposite sex and remarriage. Having been conditioned to understand that their own sexual interests are still flourishing in the fifties and sixties, they are amazed to learn that a widowed father or mother twenty years older is also interested. Since there is no set age for the sex drive to diminish, there is no set age at which remarriage is not warranted. It is thoughtless and selfish of sixty-year-old "children" to object to the desire of their elderly parent to find a satisfying relationship. There are other motives for remarriage, none of which should really disturb children—but frequently do. Longing for one's own home, a companion, and a certain amount of economic security are valid motives for remarrying at an advanced age. Unfortunately, some middle-aged children think of an elderly parent as one whose feelings have been put on a shelf to gather dust along with other relics. Undoubtedly the fear that an expected inheritance will go to a stepparent also plays a large part in the discouragement of remarriage by children. They should not overlook the practical side to this picture which might possibly alter their objections. If a widowed father marries a younger woman, he will not resort to living with one of his children, and will have someone to take care of him. If a widowed mother marries an older man, she will be occupied taking care of him and not have time to fret over her progeny.

Keeping a close and loving relationship with elderly parents can be as rewarding for middle-aged children as it is for younger children. One of my dearest memories is of Esther Turk, my husband's mother, as she mellowed into her seventies and eighties. The give-and-take between the two older generations is a reciprocal exchange of values, information, and attitudes that can warmly enrich both.

In the final analysis it doesn't matter too much whether you keep the old folks at home, close to home, or far from home. You may be a middle-aged child in the final quarter of the twentieth century, with a whole new set of adjustments to make, but if you do a good job of it, you will be making it easier for *your* middle-aged children when *you* live past the century mark.

CHAPTER XI

THE SECOND TIME AROUND

No, this chapter is *not* about second marriages, although its basic premise applies to anything you're going to do for the second time. Why not make it better—whatever it is—the second time around?

"Well," you may say, "for one thing, I'm older. How can I compete with people years younger? For another, I'm not that fast and furious. Who wants to be? And for still another, how am I going to do anything better the second time if I didn't do it the *first* time?"

If these or similar thoughts have flitted through your mind in recent years and you are past sixty, don't stop reading now.

Not long ago I ran into an old school chum I hadn't seen for years. Although she had a few gray streaks in her dark hair, I recognized her immediately. Her animated face had few lines, her figure was straight and trim, and she carried a bulging briefcase. Of course I asked her what she had been doing with herself all these years. Joan brought me up to date on her marriage, three children, and four grandchildren. Then, in a breathless rush, she added excitedly, "And you know what else? I've gone back to *college!*"

It was then I recalled that Joan had dropped out of college in her sophomore year. Now, after a lapse of almost forty years, she had taken up where she had left off. She explained that once her three daughters had left home, time seemed to pass slowly. She tried to play bridge, took golf lessons, and worked as a part-time receptionist, but she still felt restless and dissatisfied. Then one afternoon on her way to the golf course, she drove past the local college. The sight of the ivy-covered buildings, lush green campus, and clusters of young people on their way to classes stirred long dormant memories. That night she discussed the idea of going back to school, first with Howard and then her oldest daughter. They both thought it was a good idea but felt that she might not qualify after having been out of college for so many years. So Joan called the junior college the next morning and was invited to come in for an interview.

Although she found that she would have to start all over again, she registered for six credits in the spring session. The first week she felt a bit awkward and uncomfortable, but so did most of the other college freshmen who were considerably younger than she was. By the third week she gained enough confidence to raise her hand and participate in class discussion. Frequently she stopped after class to talk with some of the other students. She spent rewarding hours in the college library. She became involved in a research project.

Next year she plans to go abroad to attend a four-week seminar. Howard will join her, since he's retired and thinks it's a great way to see a foreign country, while his wife is in school. With sparkling eyes Joan added, "This time I'm going to stick with it and get my degree!"

My friend Joan is one of thousands of older students who are attending schools and colleges all over the country, some for the first time, many for the second time. Some people hesitate to enroll in high school or college courses, because they feel they will be out of place. However, the U.S. Office of Education recently reported that approximately thirty million Americans are involved in some form of continuing education, whether on a part-time or full-time basis. Some older people have returned not because they have an overwhelming ambition but because they find satisfaction in keeping their minds alert and stimulated.

If you have twenty years or more stretching out before you, now is the time to learn something new. You may feel that you can't learn new things at sixty or seventy, but scientific authorities claim that it is impossible to set definite limits to intellectual growth. Education is a life process that continues from the time of your first consciousness to its last moment.

Being sixty or sixty-five years old today is not the same kind of "old" as it used to be. And "old" is not the same for any two people. "Old" is one thing for a scientist and something completely different for a football player. The body starts to age the moment it is born, and the best-preserved one is old before forty. Athletes work furiously at maintaining their muscles, but very few improve after thirty. Research, experiment, and performance have proved, however, that the mind *can*

163

improve with age. Some powers may diminish, but others are actually accelerated. If an older person fails to learn it is usually *not* because he is too old. In most cases, it's because his desire is not powerful enough, he lacks the capacity to learn that specific thing, or he has habits which interfere with the acquisition of new knowledge and skill.

Psychological research reveals that mature adults often have a considerable advantage over younger people, mostly because of the intensity and purposefulness of their interests. Although the early twenties seem to be the best years for learning, middle age is equally as good a period for formal education. Usually a superior brain remains superior, but the average brain can improve with age if its owner is truly interested and willing to expend the necessary time and effort. Nick Bruno is a butcher who came from Naples to the United States in his teens. His uncle took him into his butcher shop, and Nick's formal education ended there. At sixty-three he decided to do something about his accent and inability to read and write English. Last year he enrolled in a night school in his neighborhood. One of his customers told me that Nick has taken recently to quoting Shakespeare while slicing meat.

Research scientists, in testing the various mental faculties, have demonstrated that some areas of the brain deteriorate earlier than others, some scarcely change at all, and others actually improve with age. For example, speed of reaction usually begins to fall off before judgment; memory is likely to be impaired before reason; creative imagination often increases. The importance of these findings to further education for older adults is noteworthy. An eighteen-year-old may acquire stenography more rapidly than a sixty-year-old, since it is mostly dependent on memory. Yet the older person will do far better in subjects like psychology and philosophy, where reason and reflection are important.

A failing memory is often accepted as a sign of old age, but I wonder why. A youngster who forgets to do something is forgiven for his poor memory; his grandfather forgets and is thought to be growing "senile." If either of them took the time and effort to remember, the result would have been the same regardless of age. Arturo Toscanini memorized the complete score of an opera in two days at the age of eighty-five. His was a superior memory, but he constantly kept it in excellent working order by using it. There are stories of prisoners serving lengthy jail sentences who committed the dictionary or telephone directory to memory. A sixty-eight-year-old night watchman memorized Bartlett's *Quotations* as he made his rounds.

There is no doubt that the essential factor in preserving memory is interest. Mature actors and actresses memorize lengthy parts as well as (and sometimes better than) young ones. One of the reasons may be that they have greater patience, experience, and motivation. Of course, youth outranks age in the speed of reactions. It is seldom important for persons over sixty to run fast; however, they can easily *read* as fast as someone half their age provided they have the same training and skill. Scientific experiments have proved that the speed of learning may diminish with age but not the *capacity* to learn. A man or woman must, of course, be *willing*, as well as able, to think. This is where the problem arises for some older people. Because they have been brainwashed into believing that everything is a waste of time as they get older, they just stop trying. If they lose the drive and excitement in living and constantly using their mind, it's just a matter of time before the whole mechanism starts to rust and finally gives out.

Think about some of the things you never got around to doing when you were young. What's to stop you from doing them now? You have the time; you have some money; you have reasonable health; you have fewer problems and responsibilities. Every day somewhere an older person with spunk and drive decides to take a crack at the "second time around." Fortunately, there are many more opportunities for the sixty-plus now than existed a few decades ago.

Larry Hayes entered medical school at the age of sixty-four, graduating with honors. As a young fellow in the medical corps during World War II he became interested in medicine for the first time, but when he was discharged from the service he went into his father's retail business where he remained until his own retirement. After years of boredom he started dipping into medical books. Now he plans to go into practice in the town where he lives, specializing in geriatrics.

Margaret Jaffee liked to design clothes for her dolls when she was a girl more than fifty years ago. She married at an early age, reared five children, and made all their clothes. When the last one married Margaret enrolled at the Fashion Institute of Technology in Manhattan, taking courses in design. While there she became friendly with one of the students whose brother manufactured dolls. Today Margaret is spending several days a week designing doll clothes for the new line that this manufacturer is developing.

Clara Bennett loves to sing and has an unusually fine contralto voice. She is frequently asked to entertain at weddings, parties, and other social functions. For years her friends kept saying, "Why don't you *do* something with your voice?" Last year, on her sixty-fifth birthday, her husband surprised her with a piano. Much to *his* surprise Clara suggested that if he took piano lessons she would take singing lessons, and he could accompany her. Today the Bennetts are in great demand at musicales, benefits, and conventions. The second time around has become an exciting adventure for this couple.

No second-time-arounder ever seems to get "mental arthritis." We may not be that successful in staving off physical arthritis (although even this condition can be relieved), but there is no need to let the mind grow rigid or inflexible. Some older people use as an excuse the fact that they have retired to a town or live in a city that has limited facilities for further learning. It's true that those living in metropolitan areas have many more opportunities for culture, learning, and trying new things. Yet, even if schools, colleges, adult education, and community centers are not available or convenient, there are still correspondence schools. The International Correspondence School, the largest in the world, has been functioning successfully for several decades. Although this learn-by-mail institute is primarily a job-training school it offers correspondence courses in a variety of subjects. There are other correspondence schools that offer cultural courses on three different scholastic levels; some lead to certificates and even degrees.

This kind of learning has the advantage of individual instruction which can be broken down into lessons at the convenience of the pupil. There is no feeling of urgency or competition; on the other hand, it does not provide the challenge and companionship of the classroom or the motivation of the teacher. Although some well-known people who were pressed for time have taken such courses, I would think that the only retired people who might be seriously interested would be those handicapped in some way.

One of the largest adult education programs in this country is the popular Great Books Foundation, originally conceived by the New York Public Library. Groups of people, under trained leaders, meet in public libraries to informally discuss the greatest books ever written. These discussions are open to people of all ages and backgrounds and usually attract those who want to lap up culture in a pleasant and unstructured way. If you know a dozen such people, all you have to do is to contact the Foundation in Chicago, Illinois, and ask for the necessary information to establish a group. The training for a volunteer leader consists of a course of nine two-hour sessions which is provided in most cities. After you take it, you will be ready to organize a group, meet in each other's homes or a room in the town library, and enjoy stimulating mental and cultural activity.

What other areas are open to older people who don't want to stop meaningful living—or who want to start it?

Only last week at a gathering in a friend's home someone posed the question, "If you were guaranteed ten more years of life what would you like to do that you've never done before?" There was a moment's silence, and then a variety of comments came pouring out. Although a few people feared they were too old or there really wasn't enough time, each told of a dream that had not materialized when he or she was younger. Pauline wanted to learn to dance. Mildred wanted to travel to places she had never seen.

Nathan wanted to play the saxophone. Hank wanted to write a novel. Libby wanted to paint portraits. Bert wanted to invent things. Sara wanted to live on a farm. Jerry wanted to become a Zen Buddhist. Louis wanted to live in a trailer. Fritzie wanted to become a blonde. Carolyn wanted to be a sculptress. George wanted to speak a foreign language. Frances wanted to collect rare volumes. Mona and Dick wanted to live in a houseboat. Pat declined to answer, saying that her choice would shock everyone present. (The group speculated that she might want to exchange her husband, or become a belly-dancer, but Pat laughingly refused to reveal her ten-year plan.) One woman in the room wistfully added a simple statement that lingered in the air after the others had finished: "I'd like to find myself."

There is not one reason that these people cannot realize their dreams provided, of course, they really want them enough. Most of the members of this group have sufficient health, money, initiative, and—barring unexpected misfortune—time to successfully carry out their goals.

Pauline can learn to dance, though she may never be a Pavlova. Mildred can travel to Africa and the Orient, though she may have to go on a carefully organized group tour. Nathan can take saxophone lessons, though he may never be a celebrity. Hank can author a book by taking a course in novel writing, or just sitting down and writing, but it may never be published. All Libby has to do is enroll in any one of a dozen different art courses given at the local museum or college. Bert can go into his workshop and start refining his unfinished inventions that have been gathering dust for years. Sara and her husband can spend a summer in New England on the dream farm of her childhood. Jerry can take a course in world religions. Louis can rent or purchase a trailer and roam to his heart's content. If Fritzie wants to find out if she will have more fun as a blonde (I did—and it *works!*) she can make an appointment at the nearest beauty salon. Carolyn's desire to mold clay into beauty can be satisfied in the sculpture courses at the Museum of Art. George has a choice of five different schools in his area that teach foreign languages. With a little research and digging in the library, Frances can learn more about rare editions and start her own collection. Mona and Dick can rent a houseboat and cruise wherever they wish. I imagine there is an adequate solution for Pat who declined to answer, provided she wants whatever it is enough. As for the woman who needed to find herself, I believe she has the intelligence and awareness to seek out the counseling therapy to make the next ten years more fulfilling than her last ten were.

What a fantastically rewarding experience it can be to find *yourself* as you grow older! How, why, or where you do it makes little differnce. *When* you do it makes all the difference. And if you are past the age of sixty, the time is *now*. The second time around can be more important than the first because you have so much more to give.

Only recently have older people started coming into their own. The great strides made in medicine and science are preventing and curing diseases which killed off their ancestors at early ages. The widespread dissemination of education and culture is helping to keep their minds alert and lively much longer. They have many more choices of environment than their forebears who lived and died in the same town. Psychological research has made it evident that every person over sixty-five has an untapped "reservoir of youth" and that the process of pushing the frontiers of age further away is accelerating. An individual at the turn of the century was ancient at the age of fifty. The man or woman of today is just starting out at fifty, deciding what else he or she can do during the next half century. Instead of hankering after youth, older persons today can be secure in the knowledge that they have a very special quality, known only to their own generation. They can use this precious quality wisely, not only for their own betterment but for the enrichment of their peers.

Whole groups of older people have decided that if they are going to live longer, they are going to fight hard to live better. They are not content to sit passively on the sidelines while their problems are pushed into oblivion by the younger generation. The three important national groups that have risen to the fore in the struggle to tackle their own problems are the American Association of Retired Persons (A.A.R.P.), the National Council of Senior Citizens, and the Gray Panthers. The A.A.R.P. and its sister organization, the National Retired Teachers Association (N.R.T.A.), boast a combined membership of over five million. The 1,400 chapters of the A.A.R.P. work to promote the welfare of their members, offering them many helpful services for a nominal fee.

The National Council of Senior Citizens is also a nonprofit organization with a membership of over three million people. Founded in 1961, its aims are to restore dignity and independence to older people through such measures as adequate income levels, decent housing at moderate prices, comprehensive health services, and low-cost transportation. Both the A.A.R.P. and the National Council have strong lobbies in Washington which keep fingers on the legislative pulse.

The Gray Panthers is the most recent movement in organizing older people to work for their own interests and rights. Formed in 1970, it is loosely organized but has attracted younger adults to its ranks who are aware that age discrimination starts early in American culture. Headed by dynamic Margaret E. Kuhn, the Gray Panthers is the least conservative of the three groups and has been instrumental in calling national attention to frauds perpetrated against elderly consumers. It refuses to be "put down by people in positions of power."

Organizations such as these and a number of others that promote the welfare of older citizens are proof positive that older persons are rapidly becoming an integral part of society.

If you feel that the second time around is as important as the first, chances are you have already joined one or more of these groups. Belonging to such organizations not only adds strength and power to their membership but increases your confidence as you grow older. This sixty-plus generation is proud of its age and does not attempt to hide it. People in this group are not waiting for younger people to get around to fighting their battles; they are fighting their *own*. For the first time in history groups of older people are beginning to make the second time around count. If you have no interests in further education, culture, religion, or travel, your field may be politics. The first time around your brand of politics may have been Democratic or Republican; the second time around you may try joining an even more challenging party—the party that gets better as it gets older.

———————

The following are the addresses of the organizations mentioned:

The American Association of Retired Persons
1909 K Street, N.W.
Washington, D.C. 20006

The Gray Panthers
Tabernacle Church
3700 Chestnut Street
Philadelphia, PA 19104

The National Council of Senior Citizens
1511 K Street
Washington, D.C. 20005

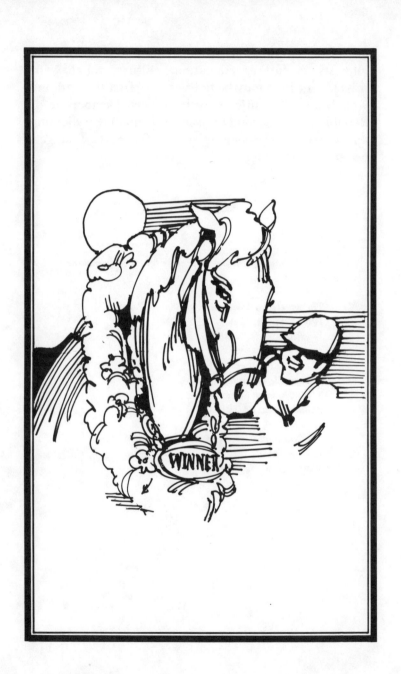

CHAPTER XII

THE WINNERS

There are countless studies, reports, experiments, statistics, journals, and books on aging. Every area in genetics, environment, diet, disease, psychology, and psychiatry has been researched, diagnosed, and evaluated so that authorities in science and medicine may understand why some people age better than others.

It seems to me that there is one common denominator possessed by all the "winners" that has never been really subjected to medical or scientific scrutiny. Grandma Moses had it when she picked up a paintbrush at the age of seventy-eight and produced a remarkable canvas. Clara Barton had it when she learned to type at eighty-nine. The French statesman Voltaire had it when he produced a play at eighty-one. Albert Schweitzer had it when he continued his work in the African jungle at eighty-five.

I call this special quality *spunk*. Lots of people have

it—young, old, poor, handicapped, fat, skinny, black, yellow, and white people. It gives their eyes a sparkle, their lips an upward turn, and their hearts a lift.

We all weren't lucky enough to know Grandma Moses, Clara Barton, Voltaire, or Albert Schweitzer, but we all know one or two spunky people who become more exciting as they get older. They may live in the house next door or the apartment upstairs.

This part of the twentieth century is furnishing constant proof that there are plenty of winners around. And most of them are at or past the age where formerly it was thought they were bound to be losers. Let's take a look at some of the present winners* who have the spunk to defy every myth about aging that has ever been perpetrated.

Last week we saw a stock company revival of an old Broadway show. The headliner was vivacious Ann Miller who got out on the stage and tap-danced as she had some thirty years earlier. Anita Loos, author of *Gentlemen Prefer Blondes* and hundreds of motion picture screen plays, recently appeared on a TV talk show. She told how she gets up every morning at 4:00 a.m., writes until ten, and then continues with work on her latest project—a musical version of one of her plays. Miss Loos is past eighty.

Arthur Fiedler, conductor and composer, has no thought of retirement at the age of eighty-one. He continues to tour the United States, Europe, and South America despite three major heart attacks since his mid-forties. There are several conductors who demonstrate this same steady determination not to quit, among them Toscanni, Monteux, and Klemperer. (Does

*Early 1976

wielding a baton keep these men in shape?) Leopold Stokowski at ninety-five has perhaps the "spunkiest" philosophy of them all: "Live in the present, never the past." As proof, he includes rock-n-roll in his repertoire.

Martha Graham continued to dance with her ballet company regularly until she was seventy-six. Now at eighty-one she is the head of a twenty-five-member ballet troupe and is still out on the stage, directing and choreographing.

The entertainment world has an impressive number of winners. Troupers like Bob Hope, Bing Crosby, and Fred Astaire are only a few who possess ageless charisma. Although I have never seen the glamorous Gloria Swanson, in a recent interview this septuagenarian actress was described as "chic and contemporary without striving to look young...a lady of wit and wisdom, full of passion for life." Actress Merle Oberon, when asked her secret of gracious aging, replied, "It's important to *think* young. Don't let your mind get rigid—about fashions, morals, anything." George Burns, a veteran comedian at the age of eighty, was awarded an Oscar for his performance in a movie about two elderly actors who stage a comeback. Screen star Lauren Bacall, past the half century mark, is annoyed with the American obsession with age. "I'm tired of all this age talk," she claims. "People act aged because it's planted on them. I'm sick of media people perpetrating age images, telling people how they are supposed to look at a certain age, how they are supposed to behave. When I married Bogie, I was eighteen and he was fifty, but that meant nothing to us ever."

At seventy-five Marian Anderson's voice has not declined in power or beauty. Perhaps giving pleasure to others, creating laughter, music, and movement are some of the reasons entertainers grow older so "fruit-fully."

Authors like Taylor Caldwell, Ayn Rand, and Rebecca West continue to contribute to the world of literature after seven or more decades of meaningful living. Margaret Chase Smith, ex-senator from Maine, leads a full and active life, traveling around the country and speaking in behalf of worthwhile causes. Margaret Mead is still involved in anthropological research. Rose Kennedy works ardently in the cause of the mentally retarded. Golda Meir, former Prime Minister of Israel, nearing eighty, is ready to rally to her homeland's call if the need should arise.

Each of these contemporary greats is meeting the challenge of getting older with spunk. Not one is lying down on the job, whatever it is, because he or she is adding birthdays. On the contrary they seem to be fighting back *as if their lives depend on it.* And maybe that's what separates the winners from the losers. Winners have recognized the universal law that to achieve one must keep active, regardless of age. This worked for Thomas Edison and Ludwig van Beethoven in the past; it works for Alfred Hitchcock and Helen Hayes in the present.

The individuals I have mentioned here have never thought of themselves as "too old" to do anything they wanted. They are winning because they take age in their stride. Many losers use age as an excuse because they have allowed themselves to be brainwashed by fear, inertia, and false images of aging.

Spunk emanates from the winner in the aging game because, psychologically, aging is as much an attitude of mind as it is a state of body. Winners actually enjoy getting older. They don't waste time moaning about what has been because they are too busy looking forward to what is going to be. They enjoy every waking moment of their lives and most of the sleeping ones. When Alexander Dumas was complimented on growing old gracefully, he replied, "Of course—I give all my time to it."

Perhaps herein lies another clue. Winners are not so much concerned with the quantity as the *quality* of their years. Since it is true that no one can avoid growing older, it makes sense to put as much zest, sparkle, color, and achievement into life as possible.

If you don't think you have a skill or talent, you may have to go searching for it. It may be hidden under years of TV watching, card-playing, or window-shopping. Grandma Moses was a simple farm woman for almost eighty years before she lifted that paint-brush. You can be a winner if you want to, but it's going to take a lot of spunk!

CHAPTER XIII

A CRYSTAL BALL: 1999

Let's pretend we have a crystal ball. Come and look with me into the year 1999. What is the picture of the older American living at the turn of the century?

Before we gaze, we must give a thought to the two predictors that stand at our elbow—the foolish optimist and the gross pessimist. The optimist will urge us to see the older person of the future as a smooth-faced, bright-eyed, springy-footed creatures gamboling joyously in Elysian fields of leisure while workworn youth bows to him in reverence, praying that he too might grow old as quickly as possible. The pessimist points to a defeated zombie crushed by pollution, neglect, and indifference, waiting his turn to enter the crowded institutions of the elderly.

The realistic image is neither of these extremes. From existing statistics, scientific data, psychological and sociological conclusions available today, we see a

181

new group emerging that will be known as the "young-old."

At the turn of the twenty-first century this group will consist of men and women between the ages of fifty-five and seventy-five. Even now, in the last quarter of the twentieth century, fifty-five is beginning to be a meaningful age marker in the life cycle because of the lowering age of retirement. With the anticipated increase in life expectancy the post-retirement period will increase to twenty-five to twenty-eight years instead of the present fifteen. Even now the majority of persons retiring are doing so earlier than required by mandatory rule, with increasing numbers retiring as soon as they can manage adequately on their retirement income. Right now, in some occupations, eligibility for pensions is determined not by age but by years of service, with the result that some people are retiring in their early fifties. With improved provision for meaningful leisure and more comfortable retirement incomes, the young-old in 1999 will leave the working world before the age of fifty. Industries will encourage people between the ages of thirty-five and forty-five to take "retirement sabbaticals." Instead of full retirement, occurring at a specific time, employees will be pensioned off at various ages for various lengths of time. During these periods, they will be free to pursue their own interests or find new ones. They will retire only when they wish, after having learned to adjust gradually to the idea of permanent leisure.

The young-old will be physically vigorous and healthy as a result of great strides in the conquest of diseases. Medical knowledge and improved health practices will produce a steady reduction in illness and mortality. Cancer and heart disease will be controlled effectively in their early stages.

The young-olds will be part of the five-generation family—as some of them are now—and will have parents living well past the age of one hundred. The trend toward separate households will have more options, with the young-olds seeking other ways of maintaining elderly parents. The anticipation of a longer period of life at a reduced income will affect monetary savings plans in young adulthood, thus assuring improved economic status later on. Economic independence will not be based solely on Social Security and pensions. The young-olds will be more financially secure and able to afford better living quarters.

The educational differences that exist between generations today will be greatly reduced, because the young-olds will continue with educational and cultural pursuits at all levels. They will take courses and go to school to keep up with the accelerated pace of the twenty-first century. They will not be content to take a back seat and permit the younger generation to run them and the country. The young-old will be highly influential in shaping political direction, actively participating in national as well as local problems. The 1999 sixty-year-olds will choose to continue working, undertake a new career, or retire to another way of life. They will display none of the stereotypes associated with the aging of previous generations. They will be found living in varied environments, having many more to choose from. Some may elect to move in an age-irrelevant society, while others will opt for peer groups of their own choosing.

The young-old will travel a great deal, moving freely because they are assured of better health, more money, and fewer responsibilities. Since they will be presenting a new and attractive picture of aging, they will be respected and welcomed wherever they go. The pendulum of age will swing more to the middle so that people will receive merit on the basis of *what* they are rather than how *old* they are.

Since there will be increased free time, the young-old will become involved in voluntary service to an even greater degree than they did in the seventies and eighties. Such service will receive as much recognition as paid labor, and in some cases even more. It will be considered a great honor to serve the community and country without monetary reward, and younger people will look forward to joining the young-old in this distinguished service.

Social and health services will be greatly improved, making it easier for the young-old to assist aging parents in solving their problems. Self-help will be taught and encouraged, but institutional care will no longer be the overcrowded last resource it was earlier.

The young-old will not only think and act differently but—due to increased health, flexibility, and attitude— will *look* different. Since they will have pride and dignity, they will move with self-assurance—heads up, shoulders back, faces mellow with young-old beauty. They will feel free to speak confidently on vital issues, knowing they will be listened to. They will be smartly groomed and coifed, not attempting to ape the young-young but adhering to a style uniquely their own.

American society will finally relinquish its youth-oriented image and place it where it belongs in the scheme of things. The young-old will assume their rightful position as a contributing segment of the twenty-first century culture. The stereotyped adage, "You can't teach an old dog new tricks," will be relegated to the archives of myths about older people, because the young-old will consistently prove it to be fallacious. They will outnumber other groups, becoming leaders and authorities in many fields formerly reserved chiefly for the young. Using wisdom and experience from the storehouse of their first fifty years, the young-old will teach youths the skills needed to join their group. It will be considered a weakness excusable only in the chronically ill and very elderly to enter into disengagement.

The young-old will live at a slower pace, concentrating on values other than acquiring material wealth and power. Schools will offer courses in preparation for the discriminating use of leisure in later life. The notion of "retirement shock" will be outmoded, since the old concept of retirement will have given way to the new one of "refirement."

In "refirement," men and women between the age of fifty-five and seventy-five will become increasingly active in the arts, contributing to music, literature, painting, sculpture, poetry, and drama. Other fields formerly the special province of the young will be enriched by participation of the young-old—television, movies, radio, and the press. They will also serve in counseling and advisory capacities to younger people in business and industry, frequently becoming reinvolved of their own volition.

The idea that youth is the only revolutionary element in society will be dissipated, because the young-old will be increasingly involved in political and social issues. A man in his sixties will fight just as vigorously for what he believes as a man half his age. There will be many organizations similar to the Gray Panthers and the A.A.R.P., and membership in them will be considered a privilege. The young-old organizations will activate and support new and ever broadening concepts for older people in the twenty-first century, and its leaders will work directly with federal, state, and community programs.

The young-old female role will undergo marked changes in 1999. Since menopausal conflicts will no longer exist, she will be able to work for reforms in which her background and experience will have meaningful value. She will play an important part in areas that deal with children, young people, and the elderly, and beyond that into broader arenas of politics, human liberation, sexuality, social and economic conflicts. She will be free to choose her own image because it will be a flexible one not necessarily associated with the roles of wife, mother, or grandmother. The woman of fifty-five-plus in the twenty-first century will look, act, and feel like a woman of forty or less. Her body and mind will be alert and vigorous because she will be at the peak of her life cycle, interested in everything around her. The males in her life at this time, whether employers, husbands, or lovers, will not be deterrents to her freedom or ambition. The 1999 young-old woman will be able to exert and assert herself with no fear that she may be categorized as aggressive. Women's liberation will be a thing of the past, because all women will be liberated.

The young-old male will also be liberated. He will be free to be whatever kind of man he wants to be. It will not be necessary for him to conceal hang-ups or stresses if he has them. He will be proud of the fact that he is sixty-five or seventy and still vitally involved in life. His mind and body will be trim and healthy, because he will want and know how to keep them that way. The young-old male at sixty-five will look, act, and feel like a man of fifty or less. He will have no doubt of his male image, because that image will have stretched to include all kinds. He will not dominate the women in his life or want to, because there will be no need for him to bolster his ego in this manner. He will continue to function effectively in any role he cares to undertake, whether as employer, employee, husband, lover, father, grandfather, or a combination of these.

In other words, both sexes in the young-old category will have achieved *human liberation* in the twenty-first century. They will use the education, experience, and wisdom they acquired earlier to make life more rewarding for both sexes. They will work side by side, pooling their intellectual, social, and sexual vitality. The "singles" will be integrated into the mainstream, not isolated because they have never married or are widowed or divorced.

A common denominator of all the young-olds in the twenty-first century will be their capacity to enjoy living without artificial stimulation. Their attitude about themselves will be positive and forward-looking because they will have a secure foundation. There will be an unbroken continuum of life's activities and frequently an increase in many of them. Marriages among the young-olds will last only if the partners in the union feel they are worthwhile.

If some of the foregoing pictures of the future young-old world seem like a chapter out of science fiction, let me mention a few salient factors. In the year 1000 B.C. in Greece, a man was aged at eighteen; in the United States in 1860 he was decrepit at thirty-five; in 1900 he rarely made it to the age of forty-eight; during the early twentieth century he was usually finished at sixty-five. The advance made in the past fifty years in the areas of medicine, nutrition, sanitation, accident prevention, and environmental control have escalated the prime or middle of life to the point where it usually ended less than fifty years ago. If the prime of life is to be reached in the sixth and seventh decades of living there is no telling where we can go. If the myths surrounding the incompetence of older people continue to be swept further into oblivion—as they are every day—the young-olds will also cease to be merely an image in a fortune-teller's glass. Improved health and economic conditions are no longer figments of the imagination for large numbers of older Americans. They are not content to accept substandard living merely because they are sixty-plus.

Those in their thirties today will be the young-olds of 1999. They will not be the pioneer generation of the new concept, because *my* generation is. However, I feel that they will do a wonderful job of making their prime of life even more meaningful than we have. After all, they will have that much more to go on, and no one needs a crystal ball to realize that.

CHAPTER XIV

DOING MY OWN THING

So far the fifth decade of my life has been the best. If anyone had told me this could be possible when I was thirty I would never have believed it. Like most other young people I rarely thought about getting older, and when I did, it was with the feeling that it happened only to *other* people. Since my own grandparents had all died before I was born, I had little association with elderly persons. When I had occasion to visit a nursing home, the sight of quavering, helpless bundles of humanity in wheel-chairs brought tears to my eyes. The few elderly people who moved and spoke had a zombie-like quality, as if they were already removed from the land of the living. Small wonder then that my thoughts of aging were synonymous with physical and mental deterioration.

It is with surprise, wonder, pride, and excitement that I have discovered quite the opposite can be true for an American woman growing older in the last quarter of the twentieth century. College graduation, marriage, and the advent of two children all took place in my early twenties. Living through World War II and its aftermath meant postponement of all personal goals for an indefinite period. The next two decades were frantically occupied with child-rearing, care of aging parents, budgeting, housekeeping, qualifying for competitive exams in the teaching field, and earning extra money as a counselor in children's summer camps. Any time I tried to snatch for myself only made me feel guilty. My role as mother, wife, student, camp counselor, and teacher left no time for *me*. I was so many things, yet who was I? What had happened to all the things I had planned to do? I was not unhappy; I had a full life. But there was one thing happening that I had not counted on: I was growing older all the time—quietly and unobtrusively perhaps, but inexorably.

And then one day about five years ago, a conversation I had with a colleague in the teacher's lounge helped to bring the whole thing sharply into focus. She was upset with the calloused reactions of the tenth-grade class she was attempting to teach. "If I hear that expression one more time I don't think I can stand it!"

Automatically I inquired, "What expression?" After all, I was accustomed to hearing a variety of adolescent aphorisms.

My colleague twisted her mouth into a wry imitation of teen-age sophistication: "I wanna' do my own thing!"

Six little words—they stayed with me all that day, floating in and out of my brain waves. They came back the next day and the next, with a peculiar insistence:

"Hey, Ruth, when are *you* gonna' do your own thing?"

I had just passed birthday number fifty. Wasn't it too late to do my own thing? And if it wasn't too late, how would I get started doing it, provided I knew what *it* was?

"Witty" sayings about getting older began popping into my mind:

> *From middle age on everything of interest is either illegal, immoral, or fattening.*
> *In youth we run into difficulties; in age difficulties run into us.*
> *Middle age is when you start eating what is good for you instead of what you like.*
> *Middle age is when you begin to exchange your emotions for symptoms.*
> *Getting older means getting colder.*

"Stop!" yelled a voice inside me. "These don't have to be true. Where is it written that doing your own thing is reserved for the under-thirties?"

I took a deep breath and advanced toward the mirror. Not a gray hair in sight, a couple of lines around the eyes, clear skin, straight teeth. *Assets:* good health, cooperative husband, adult children, good education, modest income. *Liabilities:* nearsightedness, tension-filled profession, sublimated ambitions, lack of athletic skills, tendency to care about what others think.

At the age of fifty how could I juggle them and come out doing "my own thing"? Robert Browning must have believed it when he told Elizabeth, "Grow old along with me; the best is yet to be."

That *had* to be the answer. If I could disregard growing older it would be, as the kids say, "the greatest." And that's exactly how it's been for the past five years.

It's not that I'm trying to act *younger* than my age; I'm merely acting how it *feels* to be my age. For the first time in half a century I'm really doing what I wish. I must admit that I am more than lucky to have a husband who stands by and encourages me. I don't know what I'd do if I had a staid, inflexible, Victorian-type spouse. My children have also freed me by going off and doing their own things as young adults—one in California, the other in Massachusetts. They are rather proud, I think, that their mother is working at breaking up the stereotypes about getting older.

The first one I broke up happened on the morning I marched into the principal's office to give notice that I was leaving.

"Why, Mrs. Turk, you're not *old* enough to retire. I hope you're not ill?"

How could I explain that I was leaving my job not because I was old or sick but because I wanted to do "my own thing"? I mumbled something about my eyesight and fled.

A month after I retired I found that I no longer needed my glasses to read. Yes, I am still nearsighted, but the strain caused by correcting illegible composition papers is completely gone.

Kicking over the traces starts gradually and subtly. For the first time in many years I have no boss. An alarm clock is something I use occasionally when we are traveling and the hotel desk clerk looks unreliable. Yet every day is meaningful and has a new purpose. "Doing my own thing" means doing all the things I ever thought I might want to do—and a few others I never thought about doing. It means doing things that are not limited but enhanced by being fifty-plus.

For example, I find I no longer worry about what

others think. That is a problem I now know is the concern of most people under forty. I don't mean I go around finding pleasure in saying or doing outrageous things, but if I should happen to do so, sometimes unintentionally, I find I am more apt to laugh than anything else.

Where do I do "my own thing"? I do it on the lecture platform and in the classroom. I find delight in gathering my young-old listeners and students around me and stimulating them to let their hair down. I enjoy doing a two-and-a-half-hour radio talk show on "growing older and better." I enjoy writing a column that provides a listening post for the hopes and dreams of other middle-aged people. I enjoy encouraging a group of men and women in their sixties to move with grace and flexibility, because it proves that when people get older all they need are legs, arms, and the right attitude.

I am finding that the older I grow, the easier it becomes to do my own thing—no matter what it happens to be. I choose my friends not because of their age, their social position, or their skin color but because I like them. I choose my clothes not because they are suitable or practical but because they match my mood, my body, or the color of my hair. Sometimes I buy a pair of flowered silk shoes even though they don't "go" with anything. I wear chunky rings and bold necklaces made by a craftsman in San Francisco. My purse is a huge, shoulder-strap affair built for convenience—but also for style and color.

I do "my own thing" when I entertain or when I go out to be entertained. I do not hesitate to serve on paper plates when the crowd is large because I know that my friends will eat from them anyway . . . and my "enemies" are not invited.

It's great not to be highbrow when one feels like being lowbrow, to attend a ball game in dungarees rather than a concert in velvet. It's delightful to eat pizza and coke at midnight instead of tea and toast at ten. It's fun to occasionally cuddle in a drive-in with my husband instead of in a theater.

Rather than coaching ninth graders to perform in the school assembly, I delight in cavorting across the stage, then bowing like a ham to the plaudits of the crowd. I find satisfaction in planning programs for a women's club, something for which I never before had time or interest. I enjoy being a leader when I choose and a follower when I want to sit back and relax.

I do "my own thing" when I wear a striking new hairdo or a sexy perfume. Age has nothing to do with it; all I think about is, does it look good, does it feel good, does it give pleasure to others?

Doing "my own thing" means finding new interests, exploring new fields, meeting new people. They include anything from arranging a series of rap sessions for young married couples meeting in each other's homes on Sunday evenings to hunting for Oriental artifacts across the United States. (We discovered it was more challenging to find them in the United States than in the Orient.) Traveling to new places and new climates provides countless new experiences. And they, in turn, provide new materials for the very latest and most exciting project so far—writing this book.

Being able to tell other people how wonderful and rewarding it is to grow older is more than doing my own thing. It is like carrying "a message to Garcia." It is good to tell others of my generation that there is time ahead to walk barefoot in the grass or the sand if they feel like it. There is time to stroll down country

196

lanes or climb rolling hills. There is time to write a poem in the middle of the night or a letter at dawn. There is time to read fairy tales or watch "Sesame Street" with a grandchild. There is time to enjoy an incredible sunset or a luminous moonrise.

Doing my own thing means the astonishing discovery that retirement is not the end but the *beginning*. There are always other windmills waiting out there, other lands to see, other people to know, and other books to write.

But above all there is time to love. How sweet it is to grow older and find there is all the time in the world to love! No longer any need for a snatched kiss before rushing off to work in the morning, but all the time I wish to turn to my husband of three and a half decades and say "I love you" in so many ways.

I close this book with a letter which, originally, was not meant for publication. Yet it belongs here, for doing "my own thing" was made possible mostly with the help and understanding of the man who, like me, knows that I am growing older—so what?

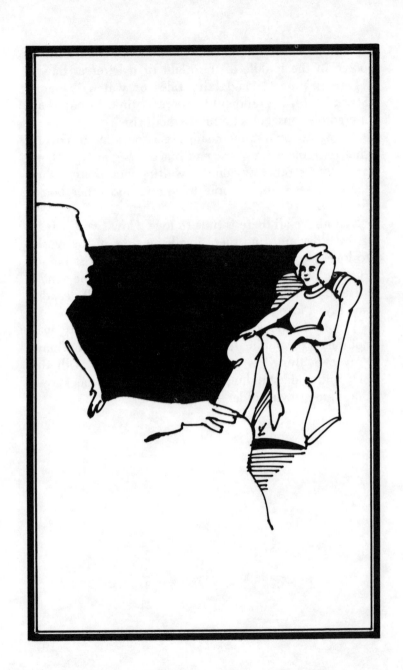

A LETTER TO MY HUSBAND—AFTER THIRTY-SIX YEARS

Darling:

The sun is shining this morning, the air is fresh and cool, and red roses are spilling their glorious color and perfume on every front lawn just as they did thirty-six years ago today. There is no anniversary card I can find in any gift shop that has space for the words I want to tell you. And though you are sitting across the room from me in your favorite chair, and I know letters are supposed to be mailed to people you don't see every day, I feel that this one is really a chronicle of a thirty-six-year-old relationship between a man and a woman.

Most relationships in a conventional marriage have conventional, expected events. Usually a young woman who married back in 1940 expected a loyal "provider," several well-behaved offspring, and a life of domestic serenity. What bride-to-be in her right mind ever looked far beyond that? I know *I* didn't. Come to think of it, I don't remember looking beyond your warm brown eyes, your strong shoulders, or your tender touch. It did trouble me rather vaguely that you had only about eighty dollars in the bank, that conscription for World War II had just gone into effect, and that employment opportunities were almost nil. But when I listened to your calm voice making the responses that Sunday afternoon in June, and when you turned to me that evening in our own home, I knew that we belonged together. There must have been countless brides who felt that way on their wedding day. But now, thirty-six years later (and wiser), I know how few wives feel the same way after living with the same man for more than three decades. *How* do I know? Because I've listened and watched and talked to some of them. They live together—many of them still do, despite the statistics on divorce of couples married a long time—but that's *all* they are doing. I tried to find out why, and I think I have. And that's why I had to write this letter—to tell you why I think we have the kind of relationship we have today.

You always let me be me; I thank you for that. You always stood by and let me know that whatever I wanted, it was all right with you. You understood that beyond being a woman and your wife, I was a person. You knew that I needed to do more than cook and clean and rear our children. And so when you came home in the evenings, you took over the care and feeding so that I could continue with courses at the local college. And when I finally achieved those hard-won credentials to teach, you encouraged and coached me through that first hectic year of transition from student and housewife to classroom instructor. When there was a need to support a sick and aging

200

mother, you never hesitated to take on still another job so that in her last years she could retain her dignity. I thank you for that.

Through the years, your tender and thoughtful acts of love have kept me in a constant glow. They go back to the days when one pair of nylons was a feminine possession of unique value, and you could not witness my daily donning of lisle stockings without suffering. Who knows what you went through to acquire a *dozen* pairs of fragile nylons (including black) and drape them over all the light fixtures to surprise me when I returned from classes one evening?

You have never forgotten to be my lover as well as my friend and husband. You have never ceased to court me in a hundred little ways, from the compliment on a new hairdo to the gift-wrapped toilet water on non-birthdays. You have never forgotten to touch me, not only with your hands but with your mind and heart. Your strength and gentleness have reached out to our children, communicating to them our relationship through the growing years into their lives as adults. Your understanding and patience have never faltered from the diaper days, through the endless childhood emergencies, into the adolescent generation gap, up to the altar and beyond. You also make the most handsome and virile grandfather I know. I thank you for that.

You have kept my passion and respect—in that order—alive all these years, by keeping your mind and body trim and flexible. I thank you for that. But, above all, I am most grateful for one of the greatest thrills a man can give to his mate of thirty-six years. It is even more exciting because it has been so totally unexpected. And that is—despite all the stereotyped myths to the contrary—you *are* getting better as you get older. Now that we are once more alone together, we have started out on still another adventure. In retirement you are continuing to share yourself with me. Your recent interest in tennis, travel, theater, transcendental meditation, and Oriental antiques, among other things, provides a never ending source of delight and wonderment for me. You do not hesitate to move into new fields and try new things, and you take me with you over new horizons. All around me I see the broadening of husbandly mid-sections, but very little broadening of sense and spirit like yours.

And by the way, have I told you how wonderful you look in your sexy new leisure suit? I thank you for making me proud and happy to be . . .

Your Wife.

SUGGESTED READINGS

Learn to Grow Old, Paul Tournier, Harper and Row, 1972

To the Good Long Life, Morton Puner, Universe Books, 1974

Stay Young Longer, Linda Clark, Pyramid Books, 1971

Getting Old and Staying Young, D. D. Stonecypher, Jr., M.D., W. W. Norton and Co., Inc., 1974

Young Till We Die, Doris G. and David J. Jonas, Coward, McCann and Geoghegam, Inc., 1973

How to Enjoy Your Retirement, John Sunshine, AMACON, 1974

Live Longer Now, Jon N. Leonard, J. L. Hofer and N. Pritikin, Aroset and Dunlop, 1974

Extend Youth, Robert W. Prehoda, G. P. Putnam's Sons, 1968

The Retirement Handbook, fourth revised edition, Joseph C. Buckley and Henry Schmidt, Harper and Row, 1971

Retire to Action, Julietta K. Arthur, Abingdon Press, 1969

The New Years: A New Middle Age, Anne W. Simon, Alfred A. Knopf, 1968

Retirement—A Time to Live Anew, Harry N. Hepner, McGraw-Hill Book Co., 1969

Keeping Young and Living Longer, Josef P. Hrachover, M.D., New American Library, Inc., 1973

The Social Forces in Later Life, Robert C. Atchley, Wadsworth Publishing Co., 1972

Creative Living for Today, Maxwell Maltz, M.D., Simon and Schuster, 1972

The Wonderful Crisis of Middle Age, Eda J. LeShan, David McKay Co., Inc., 1973

Widow, Lynn Caine, William Morrow and Co., Inc., 1974

Single Again, Dr. Howard B. Lyman, 1971

Modern Man in Search of Manhood, Thayer A. Greene, Association Press, 1967

The Incompatibility of Men and Women, Julius Fast, M. Evans and Co., Inc., 1971

Caring for the Aged, Bertram B. Moses, M.D., Doubleday and Co., Inc., 1966

The Myth and Reality of Aging in America, Louis Harris, *et al.*, A Study for the National Council on the Aging, Inc., Washington, D.C., 1975

Old Age in a Changing Society, Zena Smith Blau, New Viewpoints, New York, 1973

After Forty: How Women Can Achieve Fulfillment, Sondra Gorney and Claire Cox, Dial Press, New York, 1973

How to Stay Younger While Growing Older, Reuel L. Howe, Word Books, Waco, Texas, 1974